OPT OUT

Rethink success.

Reinvent rich.

Realize the life you want.

IF YOU LIKE THE BOOK, HERE'S WHAT YOU CAN DO TO HELP:

GO TO **OPTOUTLIFE.COM/AMAZON** AND WRITE A REVIEW

JOIN OUR TRIBE

LISTEN TO OUR PODCAST AND LEARN FROM THE INCREDIBLE STORIES OF PEOPLE WHO HAVE "OPTED OUT."

FOLLOW US

/OPTOUTLIFE   @OPTOUTLIFE

OPT OUT LIFE   @THEOPTOUTLIFE

OPT OUT

Dana Robinson

Published by Opt Out Media, San Diego, California. OptOut.media

OPT OUT is a trademark of Opt Out Media.

Printed in the United States of America.

10 9 8 7 6 5 4 3 2 1

ISBN: 978-1-7322872-4-2

LCCN: 2018945548

Cover design by Juan-Carlos Negretti via 99designs.com

Layout design by Kari Holloway via KH Formatting

Author Photo by Flavio Scorsato, flaviophotography.com

This publication is designed to provide accurate and authoritative information on the subjects addressed herein. However, neither the author, publisher nor their affiliates, officers, directors, subsidiaries and assigns are providing or rendering legal, accounting, or other professional services herein. If you need legal, accounting or other professional advice, you must seek your own professional and not look to this book as a substitute for such services. Some stories and names have been intentionally changed to preserve privacy and some creative liberties are taken in the interest of efficiency, but are immaterial in the opinion of the author.

Dana Robinson is a licensed attorney in California and Nevada, and a licensed real estate broker in California. However, his writing in this and other books and in other media is not intended as legal or real estate advice. Such advice should be specifically tailored to suit your needs. Books that provide self-help, including this one, are not a replacement or substitute for professional advice, which must be given considering your specific needs.

Join the OPT OUT LIFE tribe at www.optoutlife.com where Dana and his business partner Nathaniel Broughton share their experiences and interview successful entrepreneurs, creatives, world travelers, and people applying life-hacking skills that provide freedom and lifestyle. Find their podcast, Opt Out Life, wherever podcasts are available, including the Apple Store.

Table of Contents

Dedication

To Heather, who opted out of a normal life when she married me, and inspires me to keep opting out.

Acknowledgements

When I was about twelve years old, I was perusing the books on my parent's bookshelf and came across one entitled *The Strong-Willed Child*. My mother happened to be in the room and I asked, "who's that book for?" I was truly curious about who in our family of five children would have required a special guide-book. My mom laughed out loud and shook her head without answering. I immediately got it...*that* child was me. But, I didn't view myself as the tough one in the Robinson bunch. My sister was an 80's punk (dyed Mohawk, spider web makeup and side-eye that could kill). My brother was a subversive by age 14, but was a perfect angel at home. Why was I the one that required a how-to manual?

As an adult, I realize what made me so difficult to parent. It wasn't that I was a rebel. I was just unconventional. I did what I wanted, however I wanted. The funny thing about that is that it's actually a very easy personality to parent: you just let that kid do it their way. Life teaches them the rest. They did let me do it my way. And, life *did* teach me the rest. I'm thankful first to my parents for learning that and letting me break the conventions and be the teenager that didn't do teenage stuff. Thanks for letting me break sewing needles making surfboard bags that I could sell to the local surf shops. Thanks for letting me misuse the lawnmower mowing everyone else's lawn. Thanks for letting me abuse the woodworking tools making Christmas presents from scrap wood. For letting me rebuild the 1960 Fiat electric conversion, and the 1966 Mustang in the driveway. For letting me almost destroy the Texas Instruments computer trying to write basic programs that I thought would help me hack into important databases. Thanks for letting me mostly do what I wanted, which taught me that I could intend to do something, anything, and then just do it.

My audacious belief that I could do anything led to many hard times and life lessons. But, it also enabled me to start a business at 19, and another at 22, and to sell both when I was ready to move onto something else. By then I didn't need my parents' tacit approval, but my wife's. Heather was just-crazy-enough to marry me, and to believe that I could do anything I said I could do. Without her as my muse, I may not have done anything. I'm sure she regrets some of the things I tried (the coffeehouse is a sore subject). But, she is my sounding board, and the life-partner that I need to keep being unconventional in my life-path.

As life rolled on, my entrepreneurial experiences were enhanced by business partners. I am grateful to my first business partner George Esquivel, who has poured his life into the venture we started together in 2001, making shoes in Southern California. Our adventures with *Esquivel* span nearly two decades and the roller coaster continues today. My other business partner Cory Verner is a childhood friend with whom I partnered in an audiobook company that eventually sold to a private equity group. Our other ventures included an import-export business that brought us on some wild misadventures through Mainland China. I'm thankful for the friendship, camaraderie and life experiences that my business partners have brought into my life. So many of the lessons I've learned were through these partnerships.

My real estate ventures may not have come to pass without the shepherding of my childhood best friend Paul Donovan, who is one of the best loan brokers in California. We were both hustlers in high school, fixing cars and looking for ways to make side money to cover gas and surf wax. Now, we work together to hustle financing for real estate deals.

I am thankful to Jess Longordo, my longtime paralegal, who has been part of my many ventures and is the anchor to my law practice along with Kayla Jimenez, the attorney who does the hard work of lawyering while I write and travel.

Thanks to my sister Tiffany for her many years of support in managing unwieldy properties, and to my brother Tristan who has been a sounding board throughout my life, and a support in so many other ways.

My many mentors have been the source of personal and professional growth, including Whitney Thier, Ted Quirk, and Jim Scott.

Thanks to Nathaniel Broughton, my partner in Opt Out Life, who has been a vital part of bringing these concepts to life.

To Geoff Cribbs, who said, "just publish the damn book," I am thankful to have someone push me to just get it out there.

Thanks to Bill Mueller, my dog Monty's adoptive father. He's a killer editor and has been part of the evolution of this book. My first month in Bali, I re-worked a chapter I had started years before and emailed it to Bill. He took an axe to it, and thus began the path of writing this book.

Finally, thanks to my daughter Chloe for putting up with the entrepreneurial life and still turning out so well. I can't take credit for her awesomeness but am thankful for her lifelong patience with being part of an opt-out life.

Introduction

My wife and I sat on chaise lounges and took a deep breath. In front of us was the vast Indian Ocean. Behind us was a ring of clouds surrounding Bali's volcanic mountains, and the lush, green slopes that dive sharply toward the coast. A short Balinese man plodded our way carrying two coconuts with straws poking from the top; he wore a traditional shirt, a baseball cap, and a large grin. He probably saw our own smiles, the smiles of two Americans who just arrived in paradise.

Okay, maybe he was smiling because he was about to make a profit on our naiveté. We paid double for those coconuts, and sat with big smiles on our faces. We sat and soaked it in. And by it, I don't just mean the warm azure water, the beautiful rice fields and the delicious coconut. What I mean by "it" is the fact that we were there at all.

Just a short time before, I had been furiously answering emails and watching my phone blow up with messages from three different apps, letting phone calls go to voicemail, and driving three different directions through traffic. In short, the normal American life.

But we had done the unthinkable. We had pulled off the Great Escape. We bailed out on the rat race ... not just for a short vacation, but indefinitely.

We came to Bali on a one-way ticket.

As we sat on those chaise lounges, we occasionally sighed. We'd look at each other and laugh a little, without a word. After months of planning, we were in Bali, Indonesia, sitting on the beach holding overpriced coconuts.

I left Heather under the umbrella and took a long solitary walk along the beach. There were a few surfers out in the 80-degree water. Local children were playing in the shorebreak. A Balinese Hindu temple was silhouetted in the distance, on a short bluff at the edge of the beach. I walked toward it, feeling something I had not felt in a long time. The feeling of being free. That feeling you may have only had when school lets out for summer and you know you won't have any homework for three months. That feeling was slowly sinking in. My brain was fighting it. I was looking for problems to solve. I was looking for tasks to do. My brain was not yet comfortable without something to fixate on.

I reached the temple and walked up the stairs leading from the sand to the entrance. A sign warned that it was a place of worship and recited a dress code. I was in board shorts and shirtless. I took a moment to stare into the courtyard of this ancient structure. The temple consisted of large patio in the center covered by a high roof supported by stone pillars. The carved stone outer wall appeared to be lava rock. I imagined the time and patience of the stone carvers who created these very ornate walls from solid rock. I didn't yet know that in a matter of weeks, I would end up at a ceremony in a temple much like this one, wearing a sarong and traditional headdress.

I turned my back to the temple to survey the ocean before me, and shook my head. Yup, I was really here.

As I sauntered back to my wife's chaise, I gazed on the towering volcanoes. There was a cloud layer that appeared to be expanding. Clouds from the north were moving quickly, which was beautiful to watch.

By the time I reached Heather, I looked around and realized that the beach had become sparse. I looked up to where my scooter was parked and saw only a few bikes other than mine. We quickly gathered our things and kicked the scooter into gear.

The sun faded as we wound down a dirt path away from the beach. We passed a water buffalo tethered to a tree in a field as we crossed it, en route to the main road. Droplets hit our helmets, and Heather tightened her grip on my waist. This was a first: riding a scooter across a field under the watchful eye of a water buffalo as rain began to fall on us. It would be one of many firsts. We rode on as the sprinkles turned into drops, and the drops turned into a downpour. I wore only a T-shirt, board shorts and flip-flops; Heather, a swimsuit and sarong. "Oh crap!" she said as the rain turned into sheets. We were drenched within minutes as we sped along a cobblestone road, passing rice fields, villas, shops, and kids on bicycles. Somehow all the locals passing us on scooters wore rain ponchos. Another lesson learned.

The rain hammered our motorcycle helmets, the roar echoing in our ears. Water ran down our bodies and off the scooter to a road that was quickly becoming a river. We made a turn that would take us down the last road to our villa, and the road was solid water, flowing downward toward the beaches. I saw a tiny market with a roof that hung out enough to escape the rain. I pulled into the drive, and we both hopped off the bike and took cover. Heather shook her head resolutely, as if her helmet had the power to repel the humiliation along with a monsoon. Riding on the back a scooter in a brave new world was scary enough; the spooky downpour had only ramped up the anxiety. The water poured off the roof onto the ground around us. We didn't dare remove our helmets and simply stared at the street-river raging at our feet.

We turned to look at each other. And then it hit us. Simultaneously. We just started laughing.

We couldn't stop. We were cold and wet and we were standing there in the rain, laughing. What started as our first "real catastrophe" had suddenly morphed into the sight of each of us looking like wet cats, all soaked flesh and soggy threads hanging off our limbs, with these absurdly monstrous and alien-looking helmets perched on our heads.

And then something else hit me. No, it hit both of us. Heather looked at me. I stopped laughing and had one of those moments. I think I cried, but I don't know because water was still oozing down my face from my wet helmet. Heather smiled and her eyes welled up. "We did it," she whispered, and I immediately knew what she meant. I embraced her, our helmets bonked, awkwardly interrupting this Hallmark moment. We laughed again and remounted the bike as the flow of water down the road had begun to diminish.

We would spend the next fourteen months in Bali. During that time, I would write this book, as well as two others. If you want to hear about my adventures in Bali, you'll have to wait for another book. This book isn't about my season in Bali, it's about how you can find the freedom to live the life you want using tools that I've developed over my career as a life-hacker. I'd like to help you find a way to free yourself from the system to do what you want to do, whether that means swinging in the trees with monkeys on an island, living the posh life in a mansion, or simply owning the picket fence dream that so eludes most Americans.

You might be asking what lottery I won to entitle me to live in Bali and spend my days writing, exploring the beaches of Bali, and, well, not working. You might ask, "How do you get to do that?"

It's a fair question. The truth is that I didn't win the lottery. I didn't cash in on an IPO or sell a company. I opted out.

Bali is full of dropouts; and of course Bali isn't the only place. But there's also another, entirely separate class of dropouts I hadn't fully recognized before. I'm not talking about those who have dropped out of society. I'm referring to those of us who have opted out of the system.

Opting out doesn't require that you inherit an estate, sell a company, or win a longshot on the ponies. It starts with a shift in mentality, and then the adoption of a new set of rules that eventually give you the freedom to do this, or to do any number of other things in life that you might dream of.

How do you cut off the email circus? How do you stop the hamster wheel? How do you take the leap, break free of the rat race, and find yourself writing that book you've always wanted to write, or practicing yoga in the jungle, or surfing in the Indian Ocean? How do you disconnect from the American Dream once you realize it's a trap that is slowly sucking the life out of you, one meeting at a time?

The answer is simple. You opt out.

Chapter One:
A Confession

Before you read any further, I have to make a confession – this book is about me. But it's not an autobiography. I'm going to tell you a lot about myself, not because I want to brag, but because I'm living a life that is attainable and I'd like to show you the way. I'd like for you to understand that this book isn't written by an ultra-successful business guru. I'm a flop if you compare me to the big shots of today's business and self-help books. And that's good news for you.

I'm going to share with you many amazing things I've done. But millions of other people have probably done the same amazing things or even more amazing things. I'm not special because I lived in Bali for over a year. I'm not special because I've lived in a $2 million mansion. What makes my stories worth your time is that I've done these things unconventionally. I stole this life and I'd like to help you steal it, too.

I am a rebel. But not the leather jacket and Harley Davidson kind.

More of a life rebel. Maybe a better term would be chronic opt-out-er. Or better yet, incurable life-hacker. Regardless of what you want to call me, the point is this: I never take anything at face value. It's not always a benefit to be a rebel. It gets me in a lot of trouble. But it also gets me a life of freedom without having to cash out on an invention, or hit the Megabucks jackpot. I've gotten the big life without paying the big price, not because I'm rich, smart or special. Anything I can do, you can do better. Keep that in mind as you learn from my stories.

I've given you a snapshot of my first week in Bali. Opting out can get you that life. But it can also get you the lifestyle of the rich and famous as well (without being either rich or famous).

Before Bali, I lived in a large, historic Spanish villa on a street affectionately called "The Street of Dreams" in San Diego's jewel, La Jolla.

If you had known me at that time, you would have made some very wrong assumptions. You would have seen my $2 million mansion overlooking the sparkling Pacific Ocean and assumed that I was rich enough to buy or rent it. You'd see my cars and think the same. You'd have observed my closet full of Brioni suits (worth $3,500 each), my thousand-dollar shoes, and expensive watch, and thought I was just like any other rich asshole who lived on the Street of Dreams. But you'd be wrong.

If you came into my house, you'd have seen a painting of my grandmother over the fireplace; heiress of a massive media mogul in the 1920s. You might have assumed I was heir to her legacy. I wasn't.

On your visit to my Spanish villa, you and I might have sat by the fire sipping fine wine and smoking expensive cigars. We might have talked of business, real estate, and politics. My den, with its old-world desk and Italian leather sofa, would reek of old money, or of new money pretending to be old money. I am neither.

If you saw my life on the surface, you would think I was very wealthy. On the outside, my wife and I looked like true one-percenters. And, while I'm a lawyer, that profession is not what enabled us to live the lush life. It was a series of life hacking strategies.

I was cheating the system and breaking the rules. I stole that life ... at least in a manner of speaking. I'd opted out of the American Dream. I didn't have a house in the suburbs with a picket fence, a stable job with a big 401k, or even a typical education. I was opting out, even though I couldn't articulate how. But in opting out, I didn't forego any of the things that I wanted from life. In fact, I was empowered to have it all. I just didn't pay for it the same way everyone else does.

Now that I'm here in Bali working through those principles, I realize that the very same ideas I had back then are what enable me to live here in Indonesia. In this book, I'm systematizing things in order to help provide you, my reader, with a way of understanding and implementing the things that I spent years developing. My hope is that you'll apply these principles to develop

YOUR life's adventure, whether that means writing a book while you sip from coconuts on a hammock, or whether it means living in a seaside mansion and driving a luxury car.

This book brings you through three sections. The first is philosophical. You can't opt out until you understand what you are opting out of, and then embrace what you want to do with your own version of the Opt Out life. Second, I'll address income pillars: how to create income other than from a normal job. Finally, I'll address expense pillars: how to manage expenses in unique ways to provide a good life for you and your family.

Here's a preview of the Opt Out plan.

Philosophy

Opt out! Everything around us in society is fair game. You may have already seen documentaries that address the failures of the system. Food, Inc. teaches that the food system is a mess, with a revolving door of corporate rent seekers and government regulators who create a system that does not protect your health. You may have watched Forks Over Knives, or What The Health, which show that our meat consumption is not only massively overboard, but is linked to cancer, obesity, diabetes, and other diseases. You have probably seen at least one program like Inside

Job, that shows how the 2007 economic crash was caused by corporate greed. You may have read books such as, The 3% Signal[1], that teach about how the stock market is making money at your expense, and is not really intended to serve you as an investor.

Corporate America wants you to eat yourself into unhealthiness, and then it wants to sell you medical services. It wants you to overeat, and then sell you beautification products, services, and surgical enhancements. Corporate America wants you to work at a job you don't like, investing as much of your earnings into IRAs that pay full-retail for stock that may or may not make you any money, but always makes them a profit. Corporate America wants you beholden, enslaved and moderately unhappy so that you feed your soul with consumption of products, services, and entertainment that Corporate America sells you for its own profit.

I'd like to challenge you to rethink everything. Lavish weddings, wedding rings, and even marriage. High-priced colleges, graduate schools and training. Expensive housing, automobiles, and consumer products. Extravagant experiences, travel and entertainment. Maybe you don't need an expensive wedding ceremony. You certainly don't need a destination wedding, a destination bachelorette party, and a "Wow" factor engagement party. Maybe you don't need college; maybe you don't even need a career. You may not need to buy a house, or even own a car.

---

1 The 3% Signal: The Investing Technique That Will Change Your Life, Jason Kelly. https://www.amazon.com/3-Signal-Investing-Technique-Change/dp/0142180955

Opting out means reassessing these and, well, everything else.

Opting out doesn't mean not doing cool things! You might use my principles to have an amazing wedding that wows your family, live in a mansion that is the envy of your friends, and drive a car that makes your ego swell every time you drive. Whatever your choice, I want to empower you to have what you want, and not fall into the traps that will enslave you along the way. To do that, you'll need to understand inflation, taxes, consumerism, the value of time, and the systems that are built to prevent you from getting what you want. Only then can you opt out, and find yourself outside the system, where you can actually control your life and get what you want.

You might not want the lush life or the simple island life. Maybe you just want to get out of debt, and have more discretionary income. Maybe you feel stuck and don't know what you want, but you know you want out — out of wherever you are, and onto a life in which you have more choices, and can do more of what you want, when you want. That's the Opt Out life, too. Follow my principles and you'll figure out what you want along the way.

Whatever you want, the only way to get there is to start by opting out philosophically. Start looking at the world differently. Look at time differently. Look at money differently. Step back and look at the system. Opt Out.

Income Pillars

Once you understand the philosophical underpinnings of opting out, we'll work on finding new resources for income. I propose three income pillars to support your Opt Out life.

Side Gig

I'd like to help you get a side gig. A side gig is not a business, but rather, a means of producing additional, monthly cash flow without the investment required in a traditional business. Your side gig is a non-business, but it will also be a tool to help you get into business if you so desire.

Instead of telling you to go make more money or work longer hours, I'll show you how to use a side gig to make extra money without working harder. You'll see how people are making $400 to $4,000 a month doing something that only takes a couple of hours a week. This secondary revenue source will help you fund your new life, especially when combined with my expense strategies.

Business

Unless you have the most awesome job in the world, you want to eventually own a business. I'll talk you through strategies for how you can get into business with little or no money. The same way people throw away perfectly good possessions, they also kick old-but-promising businesses to the curb. This provides an opportunity for you to get into business where someone else has lost interest.

Real Estate

Real estate is a key to emerging from moderate poverty to financial independence. There are many books about how to get rich in real estate. This isn't one of them. My take on real estate is unique, and has attainable strategies for the regular Joe. I've owned large apartment complexes, and my stories will discourage you from trying to become a real estate mogul. But there are important tax reasons to own real estate, and real estate is an inflation-proof investment that will keep paying you until the day you die. I'm not talking about the home you live in. The house where you live is a liability, as I will demonstrate. On the other hand, owning a couple of rental houses, or a small complex, can be the key to your financial independence.

Expense Pillars

Once you understand the income benefits of the Opt Out life, we'll talk about expenses. I'm not going to put you on a diet. I want you to have more good stuff in life, but not the way that society prescribes. Here are my expense pillars.

Cashless Currencies

I'm not going to tell you to spend less. Instead, I'm going to help you access new forms of currency. In my world, there are many currencies. I have a currency called trading things of unequal value, another called swapping, and one I call shifting. The rich use these methods, and the poor do as well. So why not the middle class? Until you opt out, your only currency is cash, and you can never get ahead with cash alone.

Reduced Rent or Mortgage

If you ask your parents how to save money, they'll probably tell you to rent a cheaper or smaller apartment. My advice is not to find a smaller apartment, but to look for an opportunity — to be resourceful. You don't have to rent a smaller house or apartment to save money on rent; you should consider ways to make your residential situation work for you. I'll talk you through strategies for reducing your actual rent or mortgage without diminishing your lifestyle. Maybe you'll end up with an even better lifestyle and less outflow.

Scavenging

I promise you won't have to dig through trash cans, but you will have to find your inner scavenger, so to speak. You'll need to humble yourself enough to explore thrift stores, estate sales in wealthy neighborhoods, swap meets, and Craigslist. Because I channel my inner scavenger, I live a better life than my rich neighbors, and I don't have to pay full price for any of it. I'll show you my strategies. I'm not talking about saving beer caps to make a doormat, or dumpster diving like a freegan. I'm talking about driving a nice car, wearing nice clothes, traveling the world, having time and resources to do whatever your heart wants to do, and living your own personal definition of the good life.

So, get in and buckle up! When the ride is over, I hope you'll join me as a thief in a world full of opportunities for bold souls daring to explore unconventional means of living. If you let me, I'll help you become a subversive millionaire, living the life you want.

Chapter Two:
Reinventing Rich

What does it really mean to be rich? When I was a kid, I believed that being rich was The Lifestyles of the Rich and Famous. Yachts, country clubs, mansions, exotic cars, expensive cigars, costly wine, champagne and, of course, caviar dreams. Media feeds this in television, movies, and print. The rich have private jets, private chefs, and private trainers to get their beach bodies ready to lie on private beaches and party in the south of France. The rich wear expensive clothes and Rolex watches.

When the rich get married, they host lavish parties to celebrate their engagement, to party with the bachelors and bachelorettes, and finally for the wedding. They may even have a destination wedding in Hawaii or some other exotic destination.

The rich send their kids to private schools, private colleges, and expensive graduate schools. The rich spend their winters skiing in the Alps, Aspen or Vail, burning through money on $25 hot toddies. They spend summers in Monaco having spritz and lounging on private beaches.

Or do they? The truth is that a few people really do live that life-style. But the vast majority of people who do those things are not rich enough to truly live that way. Most are spending money they shouldn't in order to experience what they perceive as the good life. You probably view this as The Good Life as well.

That lifestyle is enticing. But it's a trap. Unless you have inherited millions, you cannot buy your way into that lifestyle. Even if you earn and buy your way into that life, you aren't actually going to love it. That's because once you have a lifestyle that requires millions, you must keep making millions to sustain it. Your private jet payment is $110,000 per month, and that doesn't include the salary for two pilots, and fuel at $2,000 per flight hour. Your yacht payment is a little less, but you'll need a larger staff to run the yacht. Your country club membership is $100,000 down and $1,500 per month, and that doesn't count the minimum amount of money you're required to spend dining at the club. Your sports cars require expensive maintenance and expensive insurance. Your horses cost thousands of dollars per month in stable fees, grooming, medical bills and more. Maybe you don't know this, but horse teeth grow fast, and horse owners need to pay a specialized technician to grind the horse teeth on a regular basis. Even the rich can attest to the fact that they feel like they are bleeding money.

Being rich isn't all that it's cracked up to be. Once you have all those expenses, then you need to keep doing something to generate the cash flow to pay for it all. Even if you make it big and buy this incredible, luxe life, you may not like the idea of what it requires to simply keep it going. Step back and consider the pressure *you* already feel to pay *your* bills each month. You have to juggle money, rob Peter to pay Paul, and, like a clown spinning plates, you do your best to keep it all balanced each month. Now consider adding a couple more zeros to your monthly problems. Your power bill is $200. The guy with the mansion has a $2,000 power bill. The rich guy isn't any more free than you are. In fact, what wealthy people often crave is something that money can't buy: freedom. Johnny Carson, the famous host of The Tonight Show, craved alone time. Most successful people want the freedom to unplug, but they can't. Rich and famous people end up feeling trapped by their wealth and fame. The rich might have all the outward symbols of wealth. But the one thing they don't often have is freedom. They don't own their time. They can't step off the hamster wheel or their world comes crashing down.

I know what you are thinking. You don't want that life. You don't need a mansion and a yacht. You don't need a private jet and a Lamborghini. You don't want a vault of collectable watches. You just want a modest house with a decent car. You want to save a little and get ahead. You want to get out of debt. You want to save for your kids' college fund.

You don't lust for the luxe life. You dream of a simpler life where you have meaningful work, do what you love, and enjoy being an agent of change in the world. Your mission in life is to give back, and to do what's right.

You are not alone. Millennials, for example, "believe that every job will be fulfilling and then can't even find a boring one."[2] You want meaning, but you also just want a decent job that pays the bills. You have student loan debt. You've got a car payment. You might have young kids or one on the way. You don't need or want a Rolex. But you want a little piece of the American Dream.

I've got bad news for you. The American Dream is dead. You aren't likely to find work that fulfills your passion. And the idea of doing what you love is a myth anyhow.[3] You aren't even likely to find a boring job that fulfills the promise of the American Dream. The system is a trap, rigged to keep you in a familiar cage. If you are reading this book, you probably already have a boring job that is both dissatisfying and earns you less than you need. Welcome to the middle-class trap. It isn't much different than the wealth trap that I described above. Both are traps. Both traps put you on a hamster wheel that leaves you feeling exhausted and powerless.

I'd like to offer you an alternative. If you are sick and tired of the rat race, opt out. You don't need to run in that race. You don't need to play by those rules. You can redefine rich, and adopt a new playbook with new rules.

You can't get ahead using the old rules. Those rules tell you to get into debt to get a proper education, and then to get a proper

---

2 Jean Twenge Generation Me: Why Today's Young Americans Are More Confident, Assertive, Entitled—and More Miserable Than Ever Before
3 Mark Cuban's take is on-point: https://www.cnbc.com/2017/09/20/billionaire-mark-cuban-says-dont-follow-your-passion.html

job and pay your taxes and buy a car and work hard until you are promoted, and then to invest your money in the stock market. And your reward for all that hard work? Well, you get to take a whole week of vacation once a year to some well-marketed destination.

So it looks like this: Work at a job you hate, medicate with expensive toys, trips and wine. Go to bed. Wake up and repeat. Check your bank account and your 401k. Calculate how much longer you'll need to keep doing this. Sigh. Do you see what I mean about never getting ahead?

If you feel stuck, well, that's the point. The system is working against you. The system relies on you, and millions like you, to shut up, work hard, and then spend what you earn medicating your mild unhappiness.

What does it mean to reinvent rich? It means that you no longer define wealth in the terms that society uses. Rich is not about your luxury accessories and name brands, or what you wear. It's not about where you travel or how much money you make. It's not about fine dining, expensive wine, nice cars and large homes. Rich is about controlling your destiny. Rich is about having more time. Rich is about making money without working. Rich is about you choosing what you want to do, when you want to do it. Rich is freedom.

For me, being rich has meant many different things. It has meant spending a year in Bali doing nothing. But it has also meant living in a seaside mansion, driving luxury cars and sipping expensive scotch. I didn't have to actually be rich by society's standards to experience these dreams. What I have that most people don't have is control over my life. That's what makes me rich, according to my definition. In order to live this life, I did not need millions of dollars. In fact, while I was living in the seaside mansion, I was anything but rich. The real estate downturn of 2008 had left me with a negative net worth. At one point, I had $10,000 in the bank. I had $3 million in debt. My properties were worth $1.5 million. I was worth -$1.49 million (that's negative $1.49 million). However, even in that situation, I was richer than most! I had control over my life and my time, and I was still able to opt out and live the good life.

I opted out of the normal approach to wealth, and redefined rich. And I lived an enviable life as a result.

Are you ready to embrace a new definition of rich? Before you can really opt out, you must let go of your old notions of wealth and success. Those old notions enslave; they use those old rules to draw you back into the system. Opt out of everything you thought you knew: money, education, work, investing, marriage, and anything else you can think of. Rethink everything you thought you knew.

Forget about finding the right job with a nice pension. Forget about earning money the old way, working for The Man. Forget about the idea of career altogether.

Let go of your need to spend money on things that make you feel good. Don't go to the mall. Don't use credit cards to buy things.

You don't need to buy a house in the suburbs with a three-car garage. Today's giant houses[4] cost more to buy and are followed by larger recurring expenses for property taxes, utilities and maintenance. Oh, trust me, you'll end up with real estate if you follow my plan. But you won't be following the typical path of homeownership. Housing bubbles won't matter if you approach real estate the right way.

You won't be putting all your eggs into the stock market either. The financial systems are rigged against you, and driven by un-tethered greed. American financial institutions are not here for your benefit. They exist to take money from you, not to make you rich. Millions of people have seen Inside Job, a 2010 docu-mentary about the late-2000s financial crisis. It showed the in-herent problems of the financial services industry and the conse-quences of that systemic corruption. Several other films have documented the financial melt-down.[5]

Opt out of the American financial trap. The financial system was decried by one of my own law professors, long before the finan-cial crisis. F.I.A.S.C.O.: Blood in the Water on Wall Street[6], a fantastic best-selling book by Frank Partnoy, tells the story of

---

4 http://www.aei.org/publication/new-us-homes-today-are-1000-square-feet-larger-than-in-1973-and-living-space-per-person-has-nearly-dou-bled/ (the median-size house has increased in size by almost 1,000 square feet, from 1,525 square feet in 1973 to 2,467 in 2015)

5 To Big to Fail. The Flaw. I.O.U.S.A. Let's Make Money.

6 https://www.amazon.com/Fiasco-Inside-Story-Street-Trader/dp/0140278796/ref=sr_1_1?s=books&ie=UTF8&qid=1512855587&sr=1-1&keywords=fiasco+the+inside+story+of+a+wall+street+trader

how Wall Street is out for its own profits over those of the investors. Even if you continue to invest in stocks, bonds, and other traditional investments, you can't just trip along blindly and still get ahead. You've got to opt out of that system, and then go back in with a new approach.7

In this book, I focus on opting out of the traditional approach to making money and spending money. But it is just as important to step back and reconsider everything else. Opt out of everything.

Opt out of the American wedding trap. Don't host a destination wedding that costs $100,000. Don't even host a typical wedding that costs $35,000.8 A permit for a ceremony on the beach costs less than $100. And why would you even consider buying an expensive engagement ring? Not only is there a correlation between the cost of the ring and the rate of divorce,9 but the subversive rich know they don't need to flash diamonds when they can create something more special for far less money. Smart people are opting out of the things that society expects when it comes to lavish weddings, rings and receptions; they're even reconsidering traditional marriage.[10]

Opt out of the American education trap. I'll show you examples

---

7 Among many options, consider, The 3% Signal: The Investing Technique That Will Change Your Life, Jason Kelly (2015).
https://www.amazon.com/3-Signal-Investing-Technique-Change/dp/0142180955
8 https://www.theknot.com/content/average-wedding-cost-2016 (Manhattan wedding costs an average of $78,464, in Arkansas it's $19,522)
9 https://www.marketwatch.com/story/this-is-how-much-you-should-spend-on-an-engagement-ring-2016-02-09
10 See, Sex at Dawn: The Prehistoric Origins of Modern Sexuality. Christopher Ryan and Cacilda Jethá (2010).

of how Americans are finding cheaper ways to get a college education by studying abroad. I'll also challenge whether you need that expensive degree at all.

Opt out of the American career trap. You'll learn how people are making money through side gigs and businesses that might not seem glamorous. The guy who makes a million dollars selling license plate covers doesn't have a cool title. But, he's got a million Benjamins that don't care.

Opt out of the American consumer trap. I hope to convince you to channel your primal hunter to find bargains that enable you to have nice things. But, you won't be shopping at the mall.

Opt out of the American diet. Sadly, many are only now just realizing that even the food and drug industries are not protecting consumers, but instead are supporting corporate interests at the expense of public health.[11] You've got to opt out of all your notions about food if you want to be fit and healthy.

Not only is the food industry making you fat and sick, but the drug industry is eagerly waiting in the wings to treat your symptoms. The medical industry is a "sickness industry," which is to

---

11 See, Forks Over Knives (2015), a documentary that shows how diseases, including obesity, cardiovascular diseases, and cancer, can be prevented and treated by eating a whole food, plant-based diet, avoiding processed food and food from animals. See also, Food, Inc. a documentary released in 2008 that examined corporate farming in the United States, concluding that agribusiness produces food that is unhealthy, in a way that is environmentally harmful and abusive of both animals and employees. See also, Hungry For Change (2016), which exposed deceptive strategies designed to keep consumers coming back to unhealthy foods.

say it profits more from treating mere symptoms than creating actual cures.

You can't diet and exercise your way out of the food industry's trap. You have to opt out. You have to think differently about food before you can escape. It may not mean that you become vegan. But until you embrace the fact that the American food system is systemically flawed, and rigged against you, you cannot find a pathway out of it.

It might be easy to blame "The Man" for everything. While it is important to see that the system is built for your failure, it isn't fair to say that you are a puppet being controlled by Corporate America's strings. What keeps most people in the rat race is simply their complacency.

Take my friend Maya, who was raised in Manhattan. She was living in Brooklyn as a 30-year-old designer, living the life she thought she always wanted. She had it all: great pay, nice apartment. Friends and lovers. She had style, and owned the latest fashions. She ate out at the hippest new restaurants and went out for drinks with friends a few nights each week.

As fate would have it, she took a trip to Hawaii to reconnect with a former boyfriend. They hit it off. She made a split decision to move to Hawaii. When I met her, she was in her fourth year as the owner of a boutique that sells surfboards, swimsuits, and even jewelry that she made herself. She reflected on her old life this way: "I made a huge salary compared to what I make now, but I also had nothing to show for it other than the latest thousand-dollar handbag." Her life in Brooklyn was one that made it easy to spend all that big salary on things that seemed to matter. She vacationed in Mexico at fancy resorts. She took trips to the Hamptons and Miami. She had plenty of designer jewelry and nine hundred dollar shoes. Those things mattered to her until she opted out.

Now she rides a bicycle to work from less than a mile away. Her shoes don't matter because in Hawaii, there's no social pressure for high heels, or even high fashion. She eats local, or cooks at home. She opted out of the rat race and lives a life that she controls, and doesn't miss the expensive purses at all. She works her shop the number of hours she wants to work. She makes handcrafted jewelry, which brings her personal fulfillment and profit. She tends her garden for organic vegetables. She's hiking, camping, and learning to surf. Financially, she's getting ahead, even while making less money than when she was in New York.

Maya didn't drop out. She opted out. She now controls her destiny. And she's awake. She's alive. She is no longer on autopilot, with her time and money slipping away into oblivion.

You don't necessarily have to escape the big city to make the shift. But the big city makes it harder because it's essentially one giant magnet constantly asking you to opt in. But, with a bit of discipline, you can opt out while living the urban life.

Take my buddy Peter. He's a programmer with a degree in computer science. He has the skills to get a job making $180,000 per year. In fact, he was in corporate America for a while. He could have stayed in that track, bought a nice house and leased a BMW. He could have sent his two kids to private school, and joined the country club. At the end of each year, he would have another $30,000 in his 401k, and would have paid down his mortgage by another $20,000. He could have worked 50 hours each week, climbing the corporate ladder and increasing his pay. He didn't want that as his future. He needed to opt out.

He started using his skills to build websites for himself and for other people. He had a unique skill for search optimization as well. He eventually landed on an idea (which I can't tell you about or he'd kill me). He then used his programming skills to build a very sophisticated website. He used his SEO skills to make that site rank very well. He set up the site to make money as an affiliate (meaning he gets a little bit of money each time one of his users clicks on a link).

As of 2017, Peter lives in a $4 million house on a golf course in one of the most expensive zip codes in the U.S. He drives a $200,000 car. He has no debt. He has no employees. He does his programming in the evening, and each morning exercises with his wife before they take the kids to school. He doesn't work a normal 40- or 50-hour week. He doesn't commute. He doesn't need a company retirement plan or a 401k. He opted out and has created an amazing life by opting out of the expected path, and it has paid off very well. He didn't move to a small town. He didn't need to unplug from the social and cultural expectations. He was able to opt out without ever leaving the big city.

However, Peter had to think differently about work, money and life. He had to spend a season living simple and investing his time into his project. He had to quit a job and leave the safety of his career.

Some people move from Brooklyn to Hawaii. Others opt out and stay right at home. Others find the Opt Out life as global citizens, like my friend Conner.

Conner was a middle-class kid in Philly who hated his life. He hated his cubicle job. In his twenties, he just could not imagine doing the same thing for 50 years, then retiring to the life he saw his parents living.

Conner has spent the past five years living in Bali and not working. He surfs almost every day. He dates beautiful Balinese girls. He hops around South Asia at-will. He lives in a two-bedroom house where he keeps a car, two motorbikes, and a large cage with three monkeys he has been rehabilitating so they can return to the wild eventually. He has no boss. He has no payments of any kind — no insurance, no car payments, no credit card payments, no taxes. Conner is living the dream.

Are you wondering how this can be done without winning the lottery, or selling a company for millions of dollars? Well, Conner didn't do either. He started his adventure by getting a job teaching English at a Balinese elementary school. Once he was in Bali, he was able to find a way to quit that job, and live a life of leisure.

How does he do it?

First, Conner has side gigs. He does consulting for people who want to live in Bali. This is an easy side gig. All he does is take an hour to talk to people who are preparing to come live in Bali, and he gets $75. He can do this by phone, computer or in-person. He's making $75 an hour in a country where his house only costs him $350 per month. Most people in the U.S. don't even make $75 an hour. If Conner consults a few hours per week, it's enough to cover his basic needs.

How did he land this easy gig? It came from another person living the Opt Out lifestyle. He met Jim, a blogger who had lived in Bali for a decade. Jim had written an ebook and then built a successful blog about moving to Bali. Jim was making money from his Bali guide and getting paid to consult with people who wanted to visit or move to Bali. In time, Jim got bored with consulting and handed it off to Conner. The consulting gig allowed Conner to quit his teaching job and establish himself as independent.

That's right. One side gig that paid $75 for an hour of consulting was enough. The reason expats choose to live in Bali is not only because it's a beautiful island surrounded by good surf. It's because Bali is cheap by Western standards. Conner's rent for a nice house is a few hundred dollars a month. His power bill is thirty bucks. His water is free. He has no insurance bills. Medical costs are incredibly cheap. It costs two dollars to fill the motorcycle tank for a week. Dinner at a high-end restaurant costs $4, and a great meal at a locally run restaurant is a buck or two. Conner can live the good life for under a thousand dollars a month. How many one-hour consulting gigs does he need to do in order to live a full life in Bali? About fourteen. That's fourteen hours of work monthly. Conner never read Tim Ferriss' book, *The Four-Hour Work Week*, but surely Mr. Ferriss would be proud of Conner.

Conner also wants the freedom to do more than just live a simple life in Bali. He wants to travel the world. He wants to spend a month at a time in the U.S. being with friends and family. He wants to do fun things, and he wants to save for the future. So, with the free time he gets from working only fourteen hours per month, he also does blog entries for people who have expat blogs. He gets paid $50 to $150 an article. Even just one or two of these per month can substantially add to his lifestyle. An extra hundred dollars a month is enough to buy two or three nights at a seaside hotel on a tiny island, meaning Conner can add more dives toward his quest for divemaster certification.

Conner is passionate about photography. And he's good at it. He used his free time to master photography and software for editing photos. Well, that turned into a side gig as well. I won't give away any more of Conner's secrets. He's making money with his photography skills as well as his consulting and writing. Combined, these provide far more than he needs, and he still owns his life. His time is his own. His photography side gig has given him worldwide travel that he doesn't even pay for and substantially more money than most people make even in the U.S. That means he's not stuck in Asia. He could live anywhere he wants, including the U.S. He chooses to live in Asia because he loves it there.

I'm sure there are many excellent books about living abroad, doing the expat thing, or taking a lengthy sabbatical. This isn't intended to be one of them. This is a book about how to get the life you want, whether that life is in Bali (where Conner wants to be) or in Phoenix, New York, Portland, or San Diego (where I want to be). The tools are the same.

Do you want to travel? That's part of the life I want to live. You don't need to be rich to travel. Do you want to work for yourself? You don't need to buy a business to become free of your boss and live an autonomous life. Do you just want to increase your financial freedom? It's perfectly okay for you to want to have more money, own nice things, and live in a nice home. Conner has his version of the good life. I have mine. The lessons in this book will give you the tools to achieve your version.

In this book, you'll see many examples of people who are living their version of the good life. Each is different. But there's a common theme that you will see in each story: No one is following the accepted narrative of American success. No one has sold a company and made millions. No one has inherited large sums of money. No one is in the rat race.

Maybe you are less interested in travel. Maybe you are more interested in quitting your job. Maybe you want to keep your job and improve your lifestyle. Maybe you want to make a big pivot with your life and reinvent yourself. Whatever your aim, you must put yourself in control. You can't buy into the system. The system wants you broke, working harder, and spending everything you make so you will keep doing it again, month in and month out.

Breaking free can lead to a life such as Conner's or Maya's. It can also lead to a life that looks far more lush, like Peter's. I've told you about my Spanish Villa on the coast (the seaside mansion in Chapter 1). I currently own a condo on the beach. I also own a four-plex in San Diego's hippest neighborhood. I drive an SL500 and have owned a string of nice cars over the past decade. I've traveled the world on extended vacations. I've had the nicest clothes, handmade shoes, expensive watches, gorgeous furniture, and a cellar with hundreds of bottles of wine. None of it came from being rich; everything came from the principles set forth in this book. I'll show you how you can have my life … and even better.

I want to help you attain a lifestyle that is not far different from the life of the rich, but even better because you'll be free. You'll work when and how you want. You'll travel. You'll own nice things. You'll have freedom and flexibility to spend a day working or to spend it at the beach. You won't need millions of dollars. You won't need to invent the next Big Thing, or get the sharks from Shark Tank to invest in your new business. You won't need to cash in on an IPO or sell a fifty-million-dollar company. I haven't done any of those things. I'm just a middle-class kid who found a way to steal the good life by breaking the rules and making up my own … by reinventing rich.

Maybe you want to become an artist. You need a pathway to opt out and give yourself the time and financial freedom to do that. You might want to RV across America for a year or two. You might want to start a charity or foundation, or spend your time volunteering. Maybe, like me, you want to travel. Or, maybe you want to just live a life that's more than ordinary. The new definition of rich means having the freedom to do these things, and it doesn't require that you actually be rich by society's standards.

I want you to reinvent what you think it means to be rich, and to create an amazing life for yourself and your family. I hesitate to tell my stories. These are my trade secrets! The same is true of the stories that I'll tell you about my friends and colleagues. I'm blowing their cover. But in the end, I hope that you will learn that you can have what you want, be what you want and live the life you want. To get there you need to opt out of the "rat race" approach to life.

Chapter Three:
Moderate American Poverty

My great-grandfather was one of the captains of industry in America at the turn of the last century. Charles H. Grasty owned several of America's newspapers in the late 1800s, including The Baltimore Evening News, The Minnesota Dispatch, The St. Paul Pioneer Press, and eventually a controlling interest in The Baltimore Sun before he retired to London and met my great-grandmother. He died in 1924 with one heir, my grandmother, who took her first chunk of cash when she came of age in 1937. The fortune included cash of about $300,000, and also a trust fund with another $300,000 in it. My eighteen-year-old grandmother ("Nana") was rich.

What was $600,000 worth in 1937? Millions by today's standards. In 1937 the average cost of a new house was $4,100, the average yearly wage was $1,780, and the cost of a gallon of gas was 10 cents. The average cost to rent a house was twenty-six bucks a month. A loaf of bread was nine cents. A new car was a mere

$760. One inflation calculator says that $600,000 in 1937 would be worth $10 million in 2016 dollars. Thus, my Nana inherited an estate equivalent to more than $10 million in 2016 money. Only half of her inheritance was in cash and half was in a trust that paid her monthly at 6%. That's cash worth $5 million in to-day's dollars and an equivalent monthly income of $25,000. I'm sure most readers can fantasize about how amazing it would be to have $5 million in the bank and $25,000 per month, forever.

Why am I not the wealthy heir to this fortune? The same reason that you can no longer buy a house for $4,100, and bread for 9 cents: inflation.

By the time my Nana hit retirement age in the 1980s, she lived in a modest mobile home. The inheritance was dissipated over the years. By the time she died, what was left of her vast fortune would not even buy a condo in San Diego. She still had her orig-inal $600,000, but she didn't have the same buying power she had back in 1940. The value of her dollars went down annually, year after year, until the value of her money was virtually worthless compared to what it was when she inherited it. The wealth of an American captain of industry literally melted away in just a few generations. An inheritance of $600,000 went from being worth $10 million in today's dollars, to a value of barely enough for my Nana to live in a single-wide mobile home. As inflation rose, her monthly income did not. That monthly payment from the trust of $1,500 per month went a long way in the 1940s, '50's and even through the '60s and '70s. It was not a fantastic income by the 1980s.

My Nana did not die in poverty, but had she lived another twenty years, she would have eroded her principal funds, and seen her monthly income drop rapidly. She would have been cutting coupons. How can one of the single richest women in the country at eighteen years old turn into an average American pensioner living on a tight budget? The answer is the slow-but-steady impact of inflation.

Imagine the same impact that inflation has on regular people, on the middle class American worker. My other grandfather was a middle-class gas company employee from 1950 through 1987. In that time, he saved and accumulated a substantial retirement in comparison to his income. He saved what seemed like a lot of money. But the value of his 1987 retirement account in 2015 was insubstantial. Between 1987 and 2015, the value of his total retirement savings was cut in half by inflation even though the total dollars in that account remained about the same.

Likewise, my father's money was earned in the 1960s through the 1980s. He made money in yesterday's dollars, and saved and invested. He retired after 25 years at AT&T with a modest pension. But in the twenty years after retirement, inflation has eroded the value of his retirement income. Even if the balance of his retirement account has grown modestly, the true value of that money has declined significantly over the past 20 years since he retired.

Inflation is your biggest financial enemy. You can see it clearly in retrospect. In hindsight, you can see that bread costs more now, as does gas, cars and houses. In order to battle inflation, you have to do things that will keep pace with it. That's not easy if all you have is a regular job and an IRA.

Just consider how much more you need to make each year to keep apace with inflation. If you make $60,000 a year today, in 20 years that will feel like $32,000 in today's dollars. To beat inflation, you need to increase your income over those twenty years so that you are making $112,000 a year just to live the same lifestyle you now have at $60,000 a year. This is the case whether you are working or living on retirement income. How are you going to do that? Most people hope for promotions, and raises at their jobs. But there's no assurance of promotions and raises. In fact, as your value goes up, the odds increase that you'll get laid off to make room for lower-cost workers. Your job is no guarantee of beating inflation.

What about investing? Can you beat inflation by pouring your money into the stock market? I'm not an expert on the stock market, or stock investing. But Wall Street may not be the most effective place to put your money if you want to beat inflation. Wall Street has a dubious history, and a pattern of making money from the common people like you and me, while making billions for a select few even when things go horribly wrong for everyone else. Thus, saving and investing is no guarantee of beating inflation either.

You have to opt out of the standard approach to saving and investing in order to slay the inflation beast. The income pillars and expense pillars in this book are intended to help you do that. You'll see how having a side gig allows you to keep making money into the future, how owning a business hedges against inflation, and how owning rental property ensures that your future is inflation-proof. You'll also find that my expense pillars will help you beat the rising cost of living.

Inflation is just one of the forces that make it nearly impossible for the average American to ever get out of the hole. No matter how much you save or how hard you work, you are stuck in moderate poverty until the day you die. Life keeps getting more and more expensive, while your income grows all too slowly. This isn't what you dreamed of, is it?

The median wage for one person in America is about $27,000 per year. About 66% of Americans earn less than $41,212. At that income, a single person will take home only about $1,044 every other week after taxes. Consider the cost of rent, utilities, groceries, and minimal transportation costs (car maintenance, gas, insurance); you're simply never going to have anything left after you pay the bills. Thus, two-thirds of Americans make just enough money to live, even though, technically, we do not consider them to be living in poverty. Anything that they want other than their basic needs will go on a credit card. They are unable to save or invest, and end up retiring in an even worse financial situation. This is not a flourishing middle class. This is not the American Dream.

I call this, "moderate American poverty." The corporate world wants you stuck living in moderate poverty. The politicians want you in moderate poverty. Most people are stranded there, hoping and praying for a miracle. But you don't need a miracle. You need to step up and take responsibility. You need to see the trap of moderate poverty and choose to opt out of it.

All of this starts by recognizing that the system is built for your failure. It is built to prevent you from opting out. The American corporate and political machine wants you be cattle. And to get out, you've gotta say, as my hero Bob Dylan sang, "I ain't gonna work on Maggie's farm no more."

But getting off the farm isn't easy. And before you can implement a plan to make your escape, you have to address the forces that keep you stuck in the system; stuck on Maggie's farm.

I see two things that keep people from opting out. External forces and internal forces. The internal forces are those that are within you. The external forces are societal, those around you. Both need to be addressed before you can successfully implement my strategies. Let's start with the external forces.

External Forces

Inertia

One of the external factors that keeps people from opting out is what I'll refer to as inertia. It's also an internal force that I'll discuss below. I'm not a physicist, of course, but I'll give you the layman's definition of inertia. Inertia is a powerful force that prevents an object in motion from changing its course. Once an object is moving, it has inertia that keeps it going in that direction unless something gives it a push toward a different direction. Inertia keeps most people stuck in modest poverty. The job. The parents. The kids. The car payments. The mortgage. The expenses that keep coming up. These forces keep us stuck in place, and make it hard to break free.

In modern American life, there is constant resistance to any change in our state of motion. We can try to change speed or direction, but doing so is a move against inertia. If we want to do something different, we encounter pressure against change. Those forces might include family and friends. It might be a spouse or lover. Those around us all expect us to do things the "right way," and that means doing it the way society prescribes. We must break free of inertia to get out of moderate poverty.

I have a good friend who was thinking about buying a property for herself. It was her first real estate purchase. Everyone around her thought she should buy a small single-family house or condo. Her mother said, "Buy what you can afford." Her former boss said, "Buy something that fits your budget." A friend told her to be sure her mortgage was no more than 25% of her total income. She was inundated with advice.

I asked her to step back and doubt all the advice she was getting. I asked why she would want to carry a mortgage all on her own when she could buy a duplex and have rent coming in from the additional unit. No one had suggested that she buy a duplex or triplex. At first, she resisted my idea. People were telling her she needed a lot of money to put down on a multiplex. They were wrong. She had no idea that she could use conventional financing and buy a multiplex with only 3.5% down. Society doesn't advertise that information. Taking my advice, she found a rather shabby duplex that she could afford with just 3.5% down. It was the worst looking property in the nicest neighborhood. She had to hustle a bit to find a lender who understood the loan for this type of property. Then, through each phase, her friends and family badgered her to get out of the deal, give it up and go buy a condo.

The purchase was fraught with problems. The house needed work. Everything went wrong throughout the two-month escrow. Along the way, her mother called to talk her out of it. Her father came down to visit to talk her out of it. Her friends said it was a mistake. Why not just buy a little condo? Why buy a duplex that needed work? Why bother with all that hassle?

Well, she ignored those external forces, and ended up paying $660,000 for a property that was worth $1 million once it was rehabilitated. It cost her less than $30,000 to buy and rehab this property. And now she gets to live in one of the units while the rent from the other unit pays more than half of her mortgage. Moreover, the tax savings from the property puts money in her pocket every year when she receives a larger tax refund.

To buy this property she had to battle inertia. Her investment of $30,000 returned $300,000. That's ten times her investment within a year. She now owns a fantastic property and it changed her life forever. But inertia almost held her back.

Inertia keeps us from making good real estate decisions. It will keep you at a job you hate or prevent you from starting a side gig. To overcome inertia, you have to fight those outside voices. You'll have to make life choices that enable you to get off the hamster wheel, and get on the path toward freedom. You need to make a deliberate choice to opt out of everyone else's ideas, and then be ready to stand firm in the face of detractors.

It isn't just your friends and family that will create external inertia. We live in a culture that is rigged for your failure.

The Man

The systems around us are not built for our success, but for our contribution to someone else's bank account. Corporate America does not want you to be happy, and certainly does not want you to have financial freedom. They spend billions marketing and advertising so that you don't feel happy; you then use your money to buy things they're selling in an effort to satisfy the unhappiness. Your money is something they view as theirs. You make it so they can have it. Buy a new car and you'll be happy. Buy that sparkly ring or a fancy watch and you'll be happy. Buy a larger television; bigger is better. Of course, you'll then be captive to ads for products that pitch to your unhappiness. Buy our products and you'll be happy!

If you can't quite afford to buy things, then corporate America will grant you credit. You can use credit cards, or borrow against your home, and use that money to buy those things you think will make you happy. In the end, you are not any happier, and you have transferred a portion of your blood, sweat, and tears to some big company's bank account. You are now poorer, with no way to get that wealth back. The business world will drain most Americans of their life's blood, leaving them with an average of $178,000[12] to retire on as they live out their "golden years," feeling powerless and wobbling on a restrictive budget.

Corporate America also wants you to have a job that pays you just enough so that you can transfer the excess to them (by making consumer purchases). This keeps you enslaved to your job, working for the same corporate America that wants you to buy its goods and invest your retirement savings in their companies. Think about it: You are their "HR," aka human resources. You literally are "human capital." You are a resource for companies to deploy for corporate profit. This is a system that wants you to work your life away for the very corporate interests that enslave you through debt and consumerism. Welcome to The Matrix.

The politicians want the same thing. They want a mass of people who are complacent in their jobs, spending their money to feed the corporate interests that fund political campaigns, and a populace placated by television and entertainment. They want a populace that hears only what the politicians want them to hear. Politicians want to be sure you are completely overwhelmed and distracted. They want you to live on the edge financially and be reliant on them for help. They don't want you to pay any attention

---

12 https://www.financialsamurai.com/median401k-retirement-balance-by-age-is-dangerously-low/

to the fact that the government is passing laws to raid social security while you sleep, while actively increasing the national debt, and eroding your financial power through inflation, essentially printing more money to fund more government and giving handouts to corporations to boot.[13] Both parties do this, and the rich get richer while the poor get poorer.

All of this makes for a system that traps people into a vicious cycle of earning and consuming. You earn whatever you can by working for "The Man." You then hand all that back to The Man in exchange for shitty consumer products and mildly entertaining entertainment, leaving you short on cash every month. In the end, you use the debt that corporate America conveniently provides, further enslaving you.

Even your stocks and investments are a vehicle for corporate America to make money. You and I are "retail" investors. That means we pay the full retail price for stock in publicly traded companies. To understand what it means to be a retail investor, think of the retail stores at your local mall. *Retail* means you pay full price for a shirt at the mall. You pay $50 for that new shirt. But the retailer purchased it for $25 at wholesale. The wholesaler paid just $7 for it from the factory. When you pay full retail, you are paying five to ten-times its core value. With stock and investments, it's just like when you buy something at the mall. Others are all making money along the way, and you pay the full retail price. When you buy a purse, the original cost might be $20. The

---

13 http://www.amazon.com/Whatever-Happened-Explanation-Economics-Investments/dp/0942617622

importer then sells the purse to a retail store for $40, and the retail store sells it for $99. The manufacturer makes money, the distributor makes money, the retailer makes money, and then they sell it to you with all those mark-ups already built into the price. You pay full price while everyone else makes money. The stock market is the same. Hedge funds, private equity and professional investors are the ones making money in the stock market. You and I, the retail investors, pay full price. We never make the type of profit that professional investors make. They buy stock at low prices, and we pay full price so that they can make a hefty profit. If you're lucky, you'll make a small return (over the long term).

It's not hard to see the external forces that keep you in moderate poverty. Corporate America enslaves people to jobs at wages that are just enough and no more. Then Corporate America sells those same people unhappiness in order to sell them products they don't need. Politicians, funded by corporations, want a population of sheep that have no time to think, no power to effect change, and no freedom.

But we can't blame outside forces for all our woes. We also are part of the problem.

Internal Forces

Internal forces are just as powerful as external forces. These come from within. Your mindset. Your attitude. Your fears. Overcoming moderate poverty requires that you understand external forces, as discussed above. You must also defeat the forces at work within you.

Inertia

Inertia is an external force as I talked about above. Inertia can be those forces that surround you and keep you from making a change. But you have your own, internal inertia as well. In our society, it is damn near impossible to deviate from the path that society expects, and that's because you adopt those views and internalize them. Kids are told to go to college, get good grades, and get a job. This prescription for success is just another trap. Today's Millennial generation is learning it the hard way. They graduate with a heap of debt and no serious job prospects.

Even those who don't go to college are given a plan that is just as bad. Get a job, and eventually get married, buy a condo, have a kid, contribute to a 401k, save their pennies, and pay their bills like a good American.

Following these paths does not guarantee success. In fact, it's often these ideas that keep us in moderate poverty. If you are honest with yourself, it isn't only the outside forces, but your own attitudes about money, success, and life that are holding you back.

You are bound by your own limitations. You can overcome the social and external forces and all the inertia around you, but if you don't change how you think about money, you can't get out of moderate poverty.

I can remember a very good friend of mine who had just lost his job. I was talking with his wife, and at one point she asked me if I thought Dell computer was a good brand. Before I could answer, she said, "I think we need to buy a new computer while we have the money." They already had a computer! Her husband had just lost his job the week before! They were thinking of buying a newer computer while they had the cash, but they knew they would need to use their cash for paying the bills while he looked for a job. So why not buy a new computer before the money was gone? I hope this sounds like terrible logic to you.

What will happen if they spend the money on a computer? Well, they obviously won't have the money any longer. This is what we call a self-fulfilling prophesy. Their perception was that to be sure they get a computer, then they should buy it "while they have the money" and before they spend the money on something else, like paying their bills. If you always spend your money "while you have it," you won't have it very long. You'll be on a cycle of never having money because you think you must spend it before it flies away. The logic is backwards. If you want to have money, you must not spend it. It doesn't vanish without help from you. Your decisions are what make your money disappear. My friend and his wife were following a pattern that is hard to break. They internalized the idea that money just flies away, and that you must spend it while you have it, or you won't get to buy what you want. Unfortunately, this is how many Americans live. They feel that any money they have will vanish quickly, so they spend it on what they want before it vanishes. And then, of course, it disappears!

Why do people behave this way? This is the inertia of consumerism. Our internal desire to acquire things without realizing that buying those things will deprive us of our hard-earned cash. Breaking the cycle of consumption is not easy, but doing so will give you the freedom to opt out.

However, consumerism isn't the only internal inertia that keeps us from financial freedom.

Time

It isn't just money that people squander without realizing it. They also squander time — another internal factor that can impact our finances and keep us from abundance.

Television. Shopping for recreation. Sports and fantasy sports. Hobbies. What do you do with your time? Most Americans trade comfort for freedom, but in the end, we are no happier in our comfort. What we really want is freedom: freedom to do what we want, when we want. But in order to reach that goal, we have to opt out of the system that keeps us in the bondage of American comfort, American pacifiers. This means reconsidering what we do with our time. In this book, I'm going to suggest doing things that will require time. To start a side gig, you need time. To own a business, you need time. You may have to trade time you would have spent in front of a screen; say, scrolling through your Facebook feed, for time to start a side gig.

You will need to embrace the idea that your time has value. If your valuable time is robbed by things that don't bring you financial freedom, then you are squandering your time. Of course, there's room for fun, and some of your time should be used for your own joy. If you surf, then surf. If you run, then run. But, don't let Facebook, television, and expensive hobbies take away your capacity to opt out and get ahead.

Fear

There's one additional internal force that will keep you from achieving financial success. Fear. Fear of the unknown. Fear of failure. Fear of what others may think. Fear will put up as many defensive mechanisms as possible. It'll make excuses. It'll give you distractions. It'll tell you, "You can't do this." It'll tell you, "Don't be stupid." Fear is a liar.

How do you fight fear? With knowledge. When I took a class to get my motorcycle license, the instructors taught that your greatest enemy on a bike is fear. Fear will paralyze you. However, if you are on a motorcycle, you cannot let fear trigger your normal flight-or-fight instincts. You cannot let fear dictate your reactions. If you do, you'll get hurt, or worse. My instructor said there is one tool that will keep fear from controlling your actions: reliance on your knowledge and skills. You must take all that you know about motorcycling and have it ready for use when the scary shit is happening. You then lean on your knowledge when fear hits. That's how you avoid getting in an accident on your motorcycle. This was not only sage advice about motorcycling, but about life. Fear will prevent you from taking the right course of action with your life. How do you keep from letting fear dictate your reactions to life? You rely on the knowledge and tools you gain from experience, education, and your mentors.

You are gaining some knowledge here with this book (I hope). But, you should read the many other books I reference, as well as additional books that help you gain knowledge to help you overcome fear that keeps you from succeeding. Some books will teach you how to manage your money. Some books will help you buy your first rental property. Others will help you start a business. Still others will help you make your business more profitable. Study them all! As for my role along your path, my hope is to free you up by helping you see that there's an alternative path; the Opt Out life.

This Way Out

If you're like most people in moderate American poverty, you know it and want out. When you finish paying the bills and can't figure out where the money went ... when you get a dental bill and have no idea how you are going to pay it. You see how much you need to save for retirement, and you're not even close. You ask yourself, "How can I possibly put $650 a month into a retirement account when I'm not even keeping up with my expenses?" Maybe you can still afford to eat. You can fill up your gas tank when you need to. But you are not getting ahead. You're treading water.

If you are in this trap of moderate American poverty, then opting out is the solution. I want to help you find your way to financial independence. To get there, you must recognize that you are stuck in a rut, and that getting out of it won't come from a lottery ticket. It won't come from dreaming big. It won't come from visualization at a new age retreat, or hearing a famous speaker preach about positive thinking. It comes from seeing the truth and taking responsibility for it. Recognizing you have a problem is the beginning, but nothing happens when you deny it. The external forces and internal forces are strong. But you can break free by embracing the truth.

Are you in moderate American poverty? Want out? The first step is to embrace the philosophy I've covered so far. The next step is to begin to implement a strategy. The rest of this book covers my strategy, consisting of income and expense pillars. Let's begin your journey toward personal and financial freedom.

Chapter Four:
Starting a Non-Business

Your first step into the Opt Out life is to acquire a side gig. In this chapter, I cover the basics of what I call a non-business, or a side gig. Then, in Chapter 5, I'll give you many examples of side gigs to engage your imagination a bit and help you find a side gig that's right for you.

When I tell someone to get a side gig, they often resist. They feel too busy. They don't think they have the time. As with everything in this book, you have to stop thinking conventionally. Sometimes you discover that the time you need is right under your nose. Here's how I got my first side gig, and how it happened when I "didn't have time."

Back in 1996, I was a law student. I had a job working ten hours a week sitting in the law library computer lab. I literally got paid to sit. Oh sure, I had to unjam the printer sometimes, but for the most part my job was to check IDs to make sure non-law students didn't use our law library. It was easy money. There was only one catch: During those ten hours, I was not allowed to do any homework. I was supposed to be working; not getting paid to do homework.

I'm easily bored. So, while I sat ten hours per week checking IDs and unjamming the printer, I started reading about HTML at my little desk in the computer lab. I was learning the basics of web programming. Making web pages on the law library computer felt easy. None of my pages were published on the Internet; I was merely building things locally on the computer and then viewing them in a browser window. Yeah, remember Netscape back in 1997?

One day a guy came through the lab, saw my HTML For Dummies® book and asked how it was going. "Great," I said. "Look here." I pointed to my monitor, which had a notepad opened with HTML code on it, and then a Netscape window that showed the page in a browser window.

He told me he was a computer programmer before going to law school. He went on to tell me that I could publish my HTML pages onto the Internet for free using my school email account. He told me to read further in my Dummies book about how to access my server space with FTP, and then he went off to start on his homework. I did as he said, and learned how to use FTP to push my HTML pages onto the Internet.

It was fun. All of those pages I had created were suddenly live on the Internet! Then I realized people would have to go to a long

URL to find my pages (in fact I think my first page was this monstrosity: http://www.acusd.edu/~danar/public_html/danarobinson/index.html)

A light bulb switched on in my head. I realized that this was how all websites were built, and that all I needed was a cool domain name and I could build a website and make some money with my newfound HTML programming skills.

I went to NetworkSolutions.com and registered a domain name. I was a smart guy, but obviously not that smart. Why, oh why, did I not register "money.com," or "law.com," or some other awesome one-word domain name back in 1996 or 1997?

Of all the potentially brilliant domain names I could have chosen, what did I register? Freelegalaid.com. Not a one-word domain name, but a three-word domain. And not a particularly profitable one at that, considering the domain name was designed to provide something for free. Not the smartest guy in the room, was I?

Anyhow, I registered Freelegalaid.com. I set out to build a website that would provide free legal information for all fifty states, and in forty areas of law. That's 2,000 pages of HTML. It was a rather large undertaking for a full-time law student. How did I find the time? The same way you are going to find the time to start your side gig. I wasn't thinking linear about time; time isn't two dimensional.

Remember, I was working for the law library. My time there was not truly "used" by my job. The job required my presence, but not all of the minutes in all of the hours that I was present. That time was waiting to be used for something that could benefit me personally. I learned HTML and Javascript and launched a website all while getting paid to sit and watch the computer lab.

That semester I took a second job that also happened to be in the same library. I was hired by a computer research firm to train law students on how to use their tools. What did they want me to do? Sit at a computer and wait for students who needed help to come by. And while I was being paid hourly by that company, I was also sitting at a computer. I had two jobs that both paid me to sit at a computer simultaneously, and both enabled me to do whatever I wanted on the computer when I wasn't helping students.

With that time, I learned how to build Web pages and proceeded to build a 2,000-page site. I intended it to be a directory of legal resources; perhaps lawyers would even contribute a little free information for users. I also freelanced for an attorney who paid me $20 per hour for research … on a computer! Yup, I was able to do that very research for $20 an hour simultaneously with my time sitting in the computer lab. There were times when I was getting paid for three jobs all at once.

Time is three-dimensional. How do you find the time to start a side gig? I found the time to start a side gig, right there under my nose. You might need to do something comparable. Your side gig will eventually make money with little effort, and give you back far more time and money than you invest. However, when you first begin, you are going to have to look for the time.

Where is time hiding in your life? I don't need to be a psychic to tell you that hours a day are being squandered on social media, television, fantasy sports, and other distractions. None of these things will bring you a dollar in the future. That's the easiest place to find time. But many people have jobs that allow them time to work on a side gig. Maybe you have a job where you sit in front of a computer and browse Facebook. Why not shift that time to researching side gigs, and learning something that'll make you money down the road?

The lesson here is about how to view time as three-dimensional and not just as a flat, two-dimensional resource. I didn't have to just sit at the computer and do nothing between students who needed help. I used that time to learn a skill and then build a website.

How did freelegalaid.com go? It had traffic immediately. Who doesn't want free legal aid? I had no idea how to make money with it. I didn't have much content either. That's because lawyers scoffed at the idea of answering questions for free back in the 1990s. They refused to provide even basic information because they thought they might get sued. Some thought it was beneath them to promote themselves through articles on the Web. I was snubbed by the largest attorney forum for even asking attorneys to contribute how-to guides and self-help articles.

I continued to nurture my little side gig, and spent the next couple of years adding content, finding resources for legal aid, and having people add articles for the site. As I built additional content, I realized that I could make a little money by posting ads on the site. It's true: You can publish free information on a website and make money while you sleep. Back in 1997, when I conceived of this site, I thought that lawyers would pay for ads. But finding attorneys to pay you to advertise their firm is complicated and expensive. It turns out, however, that you don't have to go find your own advertisers. You just need to sign up for Google's Adsense program, which allows anyone with a website to make money from Google's ad network. You don't have to sell ad space; you simply put a small snippet of code on your site, and Google does the rest. If people click on ads that display on your site, you get paid. If your site gets a lot of traffic, then you can make a very nice income from just running Google ads.

Through the early 2000's my Freelegalaid.com site was making five hundred dollars per month! It became a perfect little side gig. It went on for years, making me a steady income month after month. It required no real time, and never stressed me out.

After years of steady income, I created a new version of the site that delivered an even better informational content. I added self-help forms, articles, and resources. Adding more free information brought more traffic. More traffic brought more income! My monthly income climbed into the $2,000's and then eventually exceeded $3,000 per month. Now, can you see how I was able to take fourteen months off and go live in Bali? I still collect a nice monthly payment from Freelegalaid.com, and my ongoing investment is minimal time and it requires no ongoing financial investment.

That website is now my best side gig. It is my non-business. It generates steady, predictable cash flow without the stress of a job or the investment required to run a real business. I've met dozens of others who own similar side gigs, and I'll share a few of those stories in the next chapter. Having a side gig is one of the first steps to getting out of the rat race and beginning your new life.

My website is one of the critical tools that has allowed me to live the good life. I didn't sell a company for millions of dollars, win the lottery, inherit money, or have any kind of lucky event. I just created a website and recreated it, and kept recreating it until it began to make a steady stream of income.

Some people think they need to start a "real" business, and think a side gig is a waste of time. I disagree for three reasons. First, a side gig can be the thing that brings in money that enables you to buy or start a business. You can do both. Second, side gigs are a great way for a new entrepreneur to practice with low risk. Finally, some side gigs turn into businesses.

The next chapter will give you many examples of real side gigs, and suggestions for your own. The side gig is the most important element of the Opt Out life. Many people will start a side gig and never need to start a business. What are the characteristics of an effective side gig?

Requirements of a Good Side Gig

There are six primary things to look for:

- Low capital outlay

- Low ongoing capital requirement

- Little time required (one or two hours a week)

- Steady monthly income of two-to-four-hundred dollars with upward potential without much extra effort

- Low liability, low risk

- Low stress

Let's examine each of these.

Low Capital Outlay

Businesses typically require an initial capital infusion. If you buy a business, you have to put a lot of money on the table. All of that is at risk. If the company flops, you lose it all. If it doesn't flop, it still may take many years to get your initial investment back.

Side gigs are cheap to start or acquire. You'll see many examples in the pages that follow (and I'm working on a book that is exclusively about side gigs). A business requires investment while a side gig does not, which is why I like to think of them as non-businesses.

Low Ongoing Capital Requirement

Real businesses need ongoing capital. Side gigs do not. Once you have a real business up and running, it is not uncommon to need additional cash infusions. Banks may loan you money to grow and expand, for example, or help with the time it takes to get paid by your customers. However, your side gig should generate cash flow immediately (or close to it) and not need continual infusions of capital. In some instances, there might be expenses (such as money to buy inventory to sell), but this should be money that comes back right away.

If your side gig needs you to pull money out of savings to cover expenses, then it's not a non-business, it's a business. Not a true side gig.

Little Time Required

Real businesses demand time. A lot of time. Most businesses require the owner to be totally focused on the business. A real business will enter your dreams, wake you up early, force you to bed late, and consume all your creativity and time. That's absolutely okay. But just know that's a real business.

A side gig should not require much of your time. You should not have to spend hours daily on your side gig, especially once you are up and running. Your side gig should be something you don't have to think about for days or even weeks at a time.

The side gig can be a "4 Hour Work Week"[14] idea, but ideally a side gig requires a one-hour work week, or four hours a month. It should have the potential for growth over time with little effort.

Steady Monthly Income

Your side gig should generate at least a couple hundred dollars a month. You want it to make significant cash in comparison to time required. Let's say you follow my recommendation and create a side gig that demands only four hours monthly of your time. Even if it only makes two hundred dollars a month, that translates to $50 an hour. For most Americans, that is a remarkably good hourly rate. Don't do a side gig that only makes you $20 per hour unless there's potential for the income to increase without increasing your time commitment.

The sweet spot for many side gigs is $400 to $600 a month. And if you consider that your side gig should take four hours a month, you are now making $100 to $150 per hour for your time. I had to go to school for ten years and earn three degrees to make my time worth that much per hour. If you can earn that as a side gig, then you are making more per hour than most attorneys. Many side gigs do far better.

Low Liability, Low Risk

Real businesses have risk. Risk of financial failure. Risk of being

---

14 The 4-Hour Workweek: Escape 9-5, Live Anywhere, and Join the New Rich, Timothy Ferriss (2009).

sued. Risk of a customer not paying. Risk of employee theft. Risk of competition. The list goes on. Some risks are insurable with a general liability insurance policy. But many risks are just the risks inherent in business. Businesspeople take risks, and face those risks every day. A good businessperson is an expert at balancing risks with rewards. It is the job of the businessperson to always be considering whether the business activities and risks are worth the reward generated by the profits of the company. It is a tough balancing act.

Side gigs have little or no risk for two reasons. First, the initial capital outlay is low, so there is little financial risk to the failure of the gig. Second, the product or service that the gig entails is a low-risk activity or product. For instance, don't bring in a product from China that requires you to carry an expensive insurance policy for product liability. And don't do things that are dangerous, volatile, or have questionable legality. Keep it low risk.

Low Stress

Stress is the great American killer. You should be empowered by the methods in this book. When you are empowered, your stress level is low. Owning a side gig should be low-stress. Your job might have stress. There are books to help with that. Your business might have stress. There are books to help with that as well. When it comes to a side gig, there should be little or no stress. You should not be worried about your side gig when you go to bed on Sunday night. You should not lose sleep. You should not get angry when you open an email related to your side gig. Your side gig should not make you want to yell at your spouse or punch a hole in the wall. The goal of the side gig is to add to your life, enhance your financial condition, and pave your way to financial freedom.

Remember these requirements:

- Low capital outlay

- Low ongoing capital requirement

- Little time required (one or two hours a week)

- Steady monthly income of $200 to $400 with upward potential without much extra effort

- Low liability, low risk

- Low stress

You'll see these recur in the side gigs described in the next chapter.

Chapter Five:
Side Gigs Galore

There is a lot to see and do in Bali. While we were living there, we were quite happy to just "be." I never slept so much in my life. Some people come to Bali to see everything and do everything. They want to meditate in Ubud, climb the volcanic mountains, drive motorcycles across the island, surf in Uluwatu, and see every famous temple. I was content to get bored for the first time in my life and not feel an ounce of guilt over it.

Instead of seeking high adventure, Heather and I explored a sleepy little chain of three islands called the "Gili's." The word gili means "island" and refers to a very, very small island. The Gili's are accessible via a two-and-a-half-hour boat ride from Bali. We fell in love with the island called Gili Air ("Air" is pronounced Ay-Er, the Indonesian word for "water"), where we took our SCUBA certification course. We couldn't stop taking photos! The scene was like something out of a postcard. We knew places like this existed, but never thought we'd end up at one. It truly was one of the most beautiful places I have ever been.

The neighboring island called "Gili Trawangan" is known to be a bit of a party spot. My friend Mel absolutely loves "Gili T," as they call it. Gili T welcomes backpackers, students from around the world, honeymooning couples, and old hippies — and has a few beach bars with DJ's and dancing in the sand until dawn.

We knew Mel back in the U.S. She has a side gig that lets her spend half of her time in Bali, and the rest of her time in the States. She comes to Bali two or three times each year for a month or longer and shops for jewelry, sarongs, and other locally made items. Then she fills several large suitcases with her bounty and heads back to California to sell these items at flea markets, street fairs, festivals and events. For example, she buys rings (jewelry) made from coral, shells and other local materials. A ring, for example, can be purchased wholesale in bulk for two dollars in Bali, and sold for twenty dollars at various street fairs and events.

In the winter, she typically takes three months to go skiing, and works part-time at a restaurant so that she can cover the cost of her ski pass. She lives a simple life and is mostly unrooted. That is a perfect life for a free spirit like Mel. She has no boss. Nothing to hold her down at all. When she is in Bali, "working" is just a word she might use for days when she is riding a scooter in search of interesting things she can buy cheap and resell back home. Her side gig is her only gig. It provides her the freedom that most people only achieve when they have worked for thirty years and retire. And Mel's enjoying it while she is young and can dance on the sand until dawn on a tiny island called Gili T.

Mel was not the only American in Bali doing this type of side gig. Aaron does something similar with furniture. Ginny does the same thing with purses and dresses. They are able to come to Bali for weeks or months, accumulate the things they will take home, then make a steady income from reselling those things at a large mark-up.

Mel's side gig provides a lifestyle that fits her needs perfectly. But your ideal side gig is probably not one that requires a flight half-way around the world. Let's look at some other side gigs from friends and colleagues of mine. Let your imagination roam as you read through these, and start a journal of ideas that you'll later work through as you narrow down to your own perfect side gig.

Jim's Glue

Jim was in construction for many years. In his business, he discovered that a particular glue was necessary for certain decorative facades. He purchased the glue for many years and eventually found that other contractors needed the same glue as well. He could buy this glue in large, fifty-gallon drums for less than a hundred dollars. Other contractors only needed five gallons at a time. So Jim would divvy up the glue and sell five gallons for fifty dollars. That was five-hundred dollars profit per drum, minus his hundred-dollar cost. His net profit was four-hundred dollars per drum. Once he left the construction business, he found he could sell that same product over and over for many years. He would take a monthly trip in his truck to buy the glue, then bring it home and divide it into five gallon buckets and sell it to his customers. If he did two to four drums a month, that was an income of $800 to $1,600 a month, every month. His effort was a few hours once a month. The perfect side gig.

Cory's Studio

One of my business partners built a sound studio in his garage many years ago. It serves the purpose of producing audiobooks for one of our ventures together. It also can be used by sound engineers and producers who want to record in a small, high-end studio for blogs, audiobooks, and even musical recordings. They pay him a fee to use his recording studio. The income can provide Cory with up to several thousand dollars each month. It might be less at times, and I'm sure there are months where he has not rented the studio at all. However, this studio paid for itself in a year, and this side gig now generates a steady stream of cash flow that dramatically enriches Cory's lifestyle. This is important because Cory is also an entrepreneur. Remember that the goal is for you to have both a side gig and a business. Cory has both. His business took ten years to grow to the point where he could sell it and cash out. During those ten years, he was able to live a better lifestyle because he had the side gig money from his studio. The gig requires little time, very little ongoing capital, and doesn't stress him out.

Silent Bags

My brother-in-law Tim is a property master in Hollywood. That means he manages the props used on stage or in film. Tim operates a side gig from his garage making silent bags. What is a silent bag? In the movie studio business, the props used in film must be quiet. If you film a television show with a normal grocery bag, it will be so noisy that the sound of the paper bag will overpower the actors' voices during video recording. So there is a demand for things that are quiet, including bags. Tim innovated the first "quiet" bags, patented them, and branded them SilentBags®. He has spent over twenty years making these and selling them in Hollywood.

Should Tim turn his silent bag gig into a full-time business? Of course not. There is not enough demand for silent bags to make millions of dollars. But there is a market for enough of them to keep this side gig going for the past twenty years, and probably for twenty more. It's a wonderful niche, and it gives Tim a safe little side gig for extra cash. There's low risk, almost no capital outlay, and not more than a few hours per month are involved in this non-business.

San Diego Bottle Factory

My buddy Eric started a little side gig he calls the San Diego Bottle Factory. He takes empty wine and beer bottles and, with glass-cutting tools, turns them into drinking glasses, candles, vases for plants, and more. The products he creates are upcycled: recycled to a new and higher use. He gets the bottles for free, so his cost of business is low. He sells the glasses online, as well as at street fairs and through word-of-mouth. He enjoys good beer, so his business is a good excuse for experimenting with new and different types of beer. He gets to use the leftover glass bottle to make something he can sell for more than the original beer cost. Obviously Eric also gets to drink his beer and wine with his business in mind!

Eric's non-business follows the six requirements of a side gig to a tee:

- Low capital outlay

- Low ongoing capital requirement

- Little time required (one to two hours a week)

- Steady monthly income of two-to-four-hundred dollars with upward potential without much extra effort

- Low liability, low risk

- Low stress

Gary's Video Games

Gary was a bright young student who worked for me a few years ago. He was also a true hustler. He had found a unique side gig doing what he called "eBay arbitrage."

Arbitrage is a word used to describe taking advantage of the price difference between two markets. Basically, you find that stock is cheaper on the Nikkei Exchange than on the NYSE, then you buy on the Nikkei and sell on the NYSE, making money on the small difference in price.

My student intern Gary wasn't playing the international stock markets; he was playing Craigslist to eBay. He found that he could buy video games from sellers on Craigslist and sell them for almost double on eBay. The reason was simple: Craigslist sellers don't want the hassle of listing and shipping; they just want an easy sale and cash-in-hand, while eBay provides a world-wide market, and thus the optimal price for the video games.

Gary would run around town between school and work, buying the video games he had found on Craigslist, then go home and list them all on eBay. He made hundreds of dollars every month for just a little bit of his time.

Book Liquidator

I know a guy who bought the entire inventory of a used bookstore that was going out of business. Why would someone buy thousands of used paper books in the age of the ebook and Kindle? Because people still want physical books. His price for the inventory was pennies per book. He then listed them on web-sites, including Amazon. He set up a little table in his garage to enable him to quickly wrap the books and ship them as they sold. An investment of just a couple thousand dollars resulted in hun-dreds of dollars a month for many years.

If you've ever purchased a used book, you know that even a used, two-dollar book requires double that for shipping and handling. Take a book that may have cost my friend forty cents, and he's making five times his investment on the book itself. In addition, when he charges four bucks for shipping and handling, he only needs to pay about a dollar of that to the U.S. Post Office. The rest of the profit is his to keep.

LetterPOP

One of my own side gigs is a little newsletter-publishing website called LetterPOP. I acquired it after some colleagues decided to shut down the business that owned the software. I didn't pay much for it. In fact, I made my money back in about six months. The website made about ten-thousand dollars a year and required less than an hour each month of my time. I didn't have to be a programmer to get into this side gig. I just had to be willing to look for value where others were kicking a business to the curb. One man's trash is another man's treasure.

I could certainly invest in making LetterPOP a big company and compete with other newsletter-creation tools. But, as with Freelegalaid.com, this would require putting a large investment at risk, and spending massive amounts of my time on the business. It wouldn't make sense for me to turn this profitable side gig into a real business.

As it functions now, consider how LetterPOP fits our side-gig matrix:

- Low capital outlay

  o Six thousand dollars, all recovered in the first six months

- Low ongoing capital requirement

  o $40 per month for the server, and a little redesign work

- Little time required (one to two hours a week)

  o One hour a month

- Steady monthly income of two-to-four-hundred dollars with upward potential without much extra effort

  o $600 to 800 a month

- Low liability, low risk

  o No litigation in six years, none expected

- Low stress

  o I don't lose any sleep over the website

Side-Gig Ideas for Brainstorming

What can you do for a side gig? There are a host of things. The above stories provide great examples of things that are possible, but it doesn't stop there. You can find a hundred other ways to make side-gig money. Here are several more ideas to get your brain working:

Online Video Learning

If you have an expertise of any kind, you can publish a video educational course that you offer for sale on any number of channels. There is a rising demand for video learning, and many new websites offer great ways to learn. Some are considered MOOC's, or "massive online open courses," such as Udemy.com and Coursera. Others are simply learning portals, like Linkedin Learning (formerly Lynda.com). Needless to say, these instructional platforms require content. If you have the expertise to present your subject matter, you can create a course that makes hundreds of dollars a month, every month. Even YouTube can be a source for revenue if you create content that consumers want to watch. YouTube shares revenue with you when users watch your videos.

Arbitrage

I talked about my law clerk selling video games on eBay that he purchased on Craigslist. That is just the beginning of what you can do. Consider something you know well, and focus on buying that at low prices on Craigslist and selling it higher on eBay. How about selling used cars on eBay? I've known people who arbitrage cheap cars (buying five-hundred-dollar cars and selling them for double that), and I've known people who arbitrage exotics (buying a seventy-five-thousand-dollar car and selling it for ninety thousand). Either way, arbitrage is a great way to get a non-business that fits our model.

Other places for arbitrage include buying products at garage sales and swap meets and reselling those on eBay and Craigslist. Specialize in something you know well. For example, if you know golf, you might buy golf clubs cheap at garage sales and estate sales and then sell them for five times what you paid when you sell on Craigslist or other online forums. I know of someone who did this with mid-century modern furniture. Eventually, he was able to open a full retail store.

Amazon and Etsy

If you can make something unique, or have access to a source for unique products, you can list them online on an Amazon or Etsy store. With Amazon, you can even ship inventory of your product to Amazon and then let Amazon drop-ship your products.

With Etsy, you can make money selling handcrafted items like jewelry, leather goods, and art. You can build a store with Etsy with no technical skills; their platform is made to empower people to create digital storefronts and sell their products easily. Once you are listed on Etsy, then you'll be able to boost your traffic by advertising within Etsy. In addition, many people use Facebook advertising to promote their Etsy products.[15]

With Amazon, it can be a little more complicated. You can sell

---

15 https://around.io/blog/heres-why-facebook-ads-dont-seem-to-work-for-etsians-and-5-steps-to-fix-it/

anything on Amazon. But you will need some tutorials.[16] Products must have a SKU (stock keeping unit, that bar code you see on price tags). Typically, you would list the things you want to sell on Amazon, and then drop-ship them yourself from home. If you have a product that sells particularly well, you can ship volumes of that product to Amazon and then they'll ship it directly. They deduct their fees and pay you the difference.

A friend of mine developed a line of yoga wear that she sold on her own website. But she found that it sold better when she started listing the products on Amazon. Eventually, she also started selling her time as a consultant to help other small businesses get their products listed on Amazon's Marketplace. If you don't have the wherewithal to get started on Amazon, it could be worth your money to pay a consultant to help you set it up correctly. There are even consultants who will give advice for as little as five bucks![17]

You can still sell products on eBay as well. eBay has become highly competitive over the past decade because there is worldwide competition. However, if your products are unique, you can still make money with eBay.

---

16 https://www.lynda.com/Marketplace-tutorials/Selling-Amazon-Marketplace/176495-2.html
17 https://www.fiverr.com/search/gigs?utf8=%E2%9C%93&source=topbar&locale=en&search_in=everywhere&query=amazon

eBooks

You are probably reading this book as an ebook. That's evidence that there's a market for digital publishing. If you have something to say, write a book and self-publish. Some authors publish books that they give away in order to build a list of customers, which they can then sell products to. Others simply create useful content and sell it. When I moved to Bali, I paid fifteen dollars for an ebook about living in Bali. It was worth every penny. The book was self-published, and the author kept the entire sale price. Since no major publishing house would publish a little, fifty-page guide to living in Bali, it works out just fine for the self-publishing author. I've heard that the income from his ebook keeps him living the expat life and traveling throughout South Asia. Consider what your expertise might be, and get writing!

Content Websites

I described Freelegalaid.com earlier. That site makes money from ads. I don't have to do anything other than put some code into the site, and it runs Google ads through a platform called Google Adsense.

Can you do the same? Yes! You might not want to focus on legal aid. But if you can write anything that people want to read, you can make money online.

They say "content is king" on the Internet. If we come back to Freelegalaid.com, it makes money because it has valuable content that people want to read. If you can publish useful content, you'll make money. What do you know that will help other people? Write it, blog it, publish it, and start generating traffic. The revenue may only be twenty dollars a month in the beginning. But if it's the kind of content that people want, you'll see it climb over time and continue making you money for years into the future.

Step back and consider your expertise. You might be a project manager with a hobby of growing heirloom tomatoes. You now have a choice: either publish a blog that is helpful to other project managers — or perhaps a site that helps novices understand project management — or, consider publishing your expertise about heirloom tomatoes! Whatever you do, generate high quality content, and keep generating it week after week, and eventually you'll have a site that draws traffic and makes money. You can increase traffic by cross-promoting your blog with other blogs. You can eventually even generate additional traffic by running ads on Google, Facebook and Yahoo!

Upwork & Fiverr

For many years, there have been several websites that allow you to freelance your skills. One was Elance.com, another was Odesk. Those platforms have been rolled up into Upwork.com, a website that lets you either hire freelancers or offer your services as a freelancer. If you have a skill, you can use Upwork to offer your services and also bid on projects that people post. The website offers opportunities for almost any skill, whether you are a graphic designer, database operator, personal assistant, or attorney. You can generate additional revenue by offering your service through a site like Upwork.

Many people have gone on to build a prosperous freelance business after starting out with a side gig on one of these sites. You can begin offering services at a low rate and increase your hourly fee as your reputation grows through site-posted customer feedback.

Fiverr is a bit like Upwork, but with the unique feature that all services being offered are priced at five dollars. This may seem like such a low number that you'd never make money, but it turns out you can. You can offer a cheap service for five bucks, and then charge more for upgrades. I've paid five dollars to have someone answer a question about how to fix a macro in Microsoft Excel. For an additional ten bucks, I could have paid the guy to re-write my macro. If you want a side gig that makes easy money without the hassle of starting something like the gigs I've described above, just sell a bit of your time to make $5 to 15 (or even $25) helping people with something you are good at.

There are people making thousands of dollars per month on Fiverr. The gigs start at the standard five bucks, but can go up significantly from there. With Upwork, many people are able to make more than they would at a full-time job, and work far less.

Delivery and Driving

By now we're all familiar with Uber, the service that lets anyone use their car to become a taxi- type service. You can drive for Uber or one of its many competitors, such as Lyft and Curb. There are also delivery services that operate the same way, such as Sidecar. There's now Uber Eats, and other food delivery platforms. The gig economy is creating massive platforms that allow anyone to make money doing just about anything. You can sign up for a side gig on one of these many platforms, or get creative like Jim with his glue, or Gary with his video games, and start making side money that will empower you to continue with the other strategies covered in this book.

Ultimately, a side gig is an important piece of my strategy to move you out of modest poverty. If you want to start a business, you'll need the extra cash from a side gig to help launch or buy a business. If you don't want to start a business, then a side gig gives you an amazing way to enhance your income while still keeping your day job, or while you go vagabond the world, or live on an island.

Chapter Six:
Bootlegging a Business

Part of my strategy for helping you achieve financial independence is for you to own a business. Remember the three income pillars: the side gig, a business, and real estate. In the previous chapter, I covered various ways to get a side gig. That's the first step. The second is to own a business. In the following two chapters, I'll share some unique ways to get into business.

There's a distinction between businesses and side gigs. Obviously, a side gig is a type of business, but I like to call it a non-business. Remember the difference: a side gig is cheap, easy and risk free. Businesses take more capital to start, require additional capital to keep going and involve risk.

So why am I telling you to own a business, rather than only operating a side gig?

Great question, I'm glad you asked. It depends on what you need. For some people, a side gig or two is all they need to live the life they want. If you want to keep it simple, travel, write a book, or spend your time painting, doing photography, or throwing ceramics, then a side gig could be the ultimate solution. But what if you want to live bigger? What if you want the opportunity to make hundreds of thousands, or even millions, of dollars? If you are ambitious and willing to take risk, you probably want to do more than just a side gig. You'll want to own a business, too.

Most side gigs have a limit on how much money they can produce. As you saw from the examples in the previous chapter, side gigs often provide a steady stream of income, but that income stream is limited. A good side gig can make you four hundred dollars a month on the low end, and four thousand dollars a month on the high end. Yes, occasionally a side gig can get much larger, but it isn't common. You can't grow most side gigs into large-scale businesses. This issue is called "scalability."[18]

If you can grow your side gig into a full-blown business, go for it. But at that point the side gig ceases being a non-business, and becomes a full-on business. Most side gigs won't become large businesses because they don't scale. That means you can't easily grow your side gig from making, say, ten thousand dollars a year to making a million dollars per year. Take, for example, my buddy Cory's audio studio. If he wanted to make that side gig into a business, he would not be able to use his garage. He would need to lease a warehouse and build more recording spaces. He would need to buy more equipment. He would have more capac-

---

18 https://www.investopedia.com/terms/s/scalability.asp

ity, but in order to fill that capacity, he would need to do marketing. To do marketing, he would need to invest in more staff, and put capital into advertising. He would also face competition from other large studios, and may even have to lower his prices. It is unlikely that Cory would be able to net the same profit-per-hour with a recording studio business that he now makes as a side gig. It isn't a scalable business. As a result, it is best to accept the side gig with its limitations, and choose a different business for pursuing while you keep your side gig as just a side gig. And when evaluating what type of business to own, you don't apply the same side-gig metrics that we discussed earlier in the book.

What if you don't want to work hard and don't want to run a real business? Can you just survive on the side gig alone? Yes, absolutely. If you don't need to make $10,000 per month or $20,000 per month, and you can live comfortably on your side gig income, then do so! In fact, many people with side gigs spend their time traveling and live entirely on their side gig money (like Mel). Others look for a second side gig (like Conner), and increase their monthly income while remaining free to spend their time playing beach volleyball, or working on their art, or doing competitive dance. It's quite possible to create a side gig lifestyle without ever needing to expand your horizons to a "real" business.

However, if you are like many people, you want to get ahead financially and not just live on side gig income. That's why my income pillars include both a side gig and a business. If you already own a business, then you should still be on the hunt for a side gig. If you own a side gig, then you should be on the hunt for a business. If you are just starting out, then keep your day job, and start a side gig, like we discussed in the previous chapter. That's the best place to cut your teeth on business. Side gigs are a cheap and safe way to learn the basics of business, and establish a regular income before you take the next step.

Yes owning a business will be fraught with risks. However, once you have run a side gig for a season of life, you will be more savvy when it comes to running a business. Equally important, once you have a side gig that is working (i.e. making a regular monthly income), you can use the side gig income to support the launch or acquisition of a business.

Owning a business is a key to my strategy because most Americans don't have awesome jobs with exceptional pay. If you want financial freedom, you can't be tied down to a job that pays less than your time is worth. Most financially free people are self-employed.

Why is that? One reason is that your job has a salary cap. There is a limit to how much you can make as an employee. With a business, there's no limit to what you can make. With a job, you'll always be on the clock. No matter how much you make, you have to work forty or fifty hours every week. Self-employed people aren't bound by the clock and can make money even when they aren't working. When you work a job, you don't have many tax advantages. With a business, you can expense your car, Internet, mobile phone, home office, travel, and many other things that will put money in your pocket every month. Finally, with a business you can eventually sell it, and use that money to buy another business, or retire.

Of course, I know that self-employment is not for everyone. Even among those who have owned successful businesses, many find their way back to corporate life and they like it just fine. You might like your job and not want to quit and start a business. That's great! Don't quit your day job if you like doing what you do. If you love your job, keep it, get a side gig, and follow the other principles in this book and you'll still get the benefit of the Opt Out approach to wealth. Unfortunately, most people don't love their jobs, and are stuck in those unpleasant jobs like a hamster running on a wheel. If that's you, then you'll want to own a business.

How do you get into business? You buy one, or you start one. There are many books on both subjects. What I'd like to do is offer you my take on how to buy or start a business the Opt Out way, with as little money as possible. Here we'll look at how to buy a business when you don't have much money. I call that "bootlegging" a business (stealing a business). In the next chapter, I'll cover starting a business cheaply, or what I call "bootstrapping" (starting from scratch).

Let's start with bootlegging; taking over an existing business instead of starting from scratch. The term bootlegging originated in the late 19th century to describe the smugglers' practice of concealing bottles in their boots. It has come to mean something done illegally. I like the word because it's dramatic, but I'm not actually going to ask you to do anything illegal. It's a metaphor for finding a great deal on a business, or finding ways to buy a business without using much money.

Most people don't think they can buy a business because they don't have the money on-hand. That's because most people think the opt-in way, rather than the Opt Out way. Remember how I explained paying "full retail" earlier? Most people who need a pair of shoes go to the mall and pay full retail. As a result, they end up over-paying for everything. They over-pay for clothing, cars, housing, and stock in their IRA. That same mentality leads people to believe that they can't buy a business because they don't have enough money.

What if you don't have any money, or so little you can't imagine that it would buy a business? Can you even buy an existing business and become self-employed when you don't have a lot of cash? The answer is yes. You can basically steal a business by taking over a business without any money out of your pocket.

Of course, a little cash is useful. However, stop thinking of cash as the only currency. (You'll learn in Chapter 11 about non-cash currencies.) Often, non-cash currencies are even more valuable than your cash.

Even if you have cash, you don't need to use all of it to buy a business. You can preserve some of your cash for growing your new business, and only use *some* of your cash as a down payment on the business. That's right. You don't need to pay the entire purchase price when you buy a business. Almost every business I have bought or sold has had a significant "carry-back" of part of the purchase price. That means the buyer does not pay for the business in full, up front. The buyer pays some portion of the purchase price as a down payment, and then the seller holds a promissory note for the remaining balance. Payments are then made over time. Many businesses can be purchased with no down payment at all, with the entire purchase price paid over time.

To bootleg a business, you must start by understanding that you have three currencies available to you: current cash, non-cash currencies, and future cash. You know what current cash is; that's what you have in your bank account (or stuffed in your mattress). Current cash also includes money you can draw from, such as borrowing against your 401k, or even a bank loan.

Non-cash currencies are currencies you can draw from that don't require any cash. For example, trading your time. I'll soon give you an example of how I worked for free for a month to buy a business. That didn't require any cash at all. I used a cashless currency.

Future cash is the cash that the business will make in the future. It's not your cash — yet. It's cash that the company will generate after you buy it. The best deal you can get is one where you pay for the business with future cash. When you use future cash, you are actually getting a business for free because you will use the income of the business itself to make the payments. Here's a real-life example.

Simple Steps: How to Buy a Business with Little Money Down

George purchased a property management business for $200,000. The business was making the previous owner $70,000 per year. George knew that he could increase the income with a few small changes, and cut expenses immediately after he purchased the business. He would easily make $120,000 per year if his plan worked. He purchased the business on a two-year promissory note. He put a little money down, and then was obligated to pay the rest of the note within two years. He then took over the company, reduced expenses as planned, increased income and paid off the business in less than two years with the money coming from the business itself. The purchase was almost entirely funded by the income of the business. And once he owned the business, he could draw a $120,000 per year salary for himself. The previous owner was happy with the $200,000 and moved on to do other things.

Do you see how George "stole" this business? It only cost George a little bit of cash, and then the rest was paid from the business itself. He used future cash, money from the business itself. It might seem crazy, but it's commonly done. In fact, large investment organizations called private equity groups do the very same thing for every company they acquire. You can do it, too, on a smaller scale. Here's an example of how private equity firms buy businesses and use very little of their own cash.

Cloverdale Capital approaches a small jewelry company, Jenny's

Jewelry. The current owner, Jenny, is ready to retire. Her business is 25 years old, and has $2 million in annual sales. Her net profit is about $250,000. Cloverdale Capital is willing to pay four times her profit, which is $1 million. Jenny is ecstatic. She gets to make $1 million and then retire! But Cloverdale Capital doesn't simply write a check for $1 million and hand it to Jenny. Cloverdale Capital is going to pay $500,000 up front, and then make payments on the remaining $500,000. And get this: Cloverdale Capital is going to borrow $500,000 from a bank for their down payment.

Think about that. A bank will give Cloverdale Capital the down payment with a loan against the very assets of the business (Jenny's Jewelry) it's buying. So how much is Cloverdale Capital really paying to acquire this business that already has $2 million in annual sales? Nothing. Do you see? Cloverdale Capital is buying the jewelry business by borrowing against that business' assets for the down payment and then paying Jenny the remainder out of the income of her own business. It is paying entirely *future cash*, allowing Cloverdale Capital to preserve its own cash for other purposes. Cloverdale Capital is "stealing" Jenny's Jewelry! It's fair. It's legal. It's just "bootlegging" into business, rather than writing a check. Big investment companies do this every day. And you can do it too.

This seems too easy, right? Well, it will require you to work hard to find the right opportunity. In order to find a business to bootleg, you have to be willing to look at companies that other people are passing on. Warren Buffett has been quoted that he has a "cigar butt" approach to investing.[19] That is, he wants a cigar butt that still has some unused portion left that he gets to take advantage of for free. No one else wants the cigar butt. They think it's icky. They are ready to throw it away. People toss perfectly good possessions to the curb, and they do the same with businesses.

If you want to steal a business, you must be willing to take advantage of the fact that someone else wants to get rid of it. It's their trash. Want a business for cheap or free? Think half-smoked cigar.

How do you find a business like this? It sounds impossible, right? It's not. There are many businesses in bad shape. Businesses are operated by humans, and humans are prone to encounter obstacles that impact their businesses. Death, divorce, mismanagement, financial dilemmas, laziness, and many other things cause businesses to teeter. That means you have a great chance of finding a distressed business. To find a business that someone else will give you for free or cheap, you need to find an owner who is desperate, tired, or ambivalent. In most of these cases, you will find that the company is dysfunctional. But that's okay! In fact, badly run companies are not only the best bargains, but they can be the easiest to improve with small changes. Whatever the condition of the company, you can sort through the mess and clean

---

19 http://www.businessinsider.com/warren-buffett-and-discarded-cigar-butt-2015-2

it up later.

Shopping for a business of this type is a bit like shopping at thrift stores versus going to the mall. I'm an advocate of thrift stores, as you will see in Chapter 10. Get that analogy into your head: You are no longer shopping at the mall and paying full retail when it comes to finding and buying clothes, investing in stock, buying a car, or in this case acquiring an entire business. You are digging through the scraps for something kicked to the curb, something damaged, something used and abused.

Let me tell you a story about one of the businesses I once bootlegged.

I was a young attorney, and had developed a rapport with a client who owned several businesses. This client was in my office and we were working through troubles with one of his ventures. After dealing with the issue at hand, I asked him, "How many businesses do you have?"

"Too many" he replied with his Texas drawl.

"List them," I said. "I'm not billing you right now, this is just for personal edification."

"Damn lawyers," he said, "you better not be billing my ass for asking personal questions, ha!"

He leaned back and thought for a moment. Then he proceeded to list four companies he owned or controlled. "Well there's those four, but then I also have the nursery, so that's five."

"You have a pre-school or something?" I asked.

"Ha! No, no. I have a plant nursery. I hate that business. You want it?" he asked.

I paused for a minute and said, "Okay." He literally pulled the keys out of his pocket and handed them to me and shook my hand as fast as he could.

I should have consulted my wife. I should have probably said no. I was a full-time attorney, for god's sake! But I somehow knew that this was one of those rare opportunities to score an incredible deal. I didn't want the opportunity to pass.

"It's yours," he said. "I'd better get out of here before you change your mind."

He laughed as he waltzed out of my office.

Why did the owner of the nursery give it to me for nothing? He was tired and ambivalent. He wasn't making a profit. He couldn't see a pathway to easily turn the company around. He had four other businesses to deal with. His other businesses were going well, making this one a distraction from better opportunities.

A week later, a box showed up at the office with all the records of the business, and a disk with the Quickbooks file. I decided to do a bit of further diligence, just to be sure I wasn't making the mistake of a lifetime. It turned out that the bank account had cash in it. There was one employee. There was just enough income to pay the current expenses. It felt pretty good so far.

I went to the property and met my new employee and looked around. There were signs of neglect. But it seemed like it could be a functional business. The location was perfect, with freeway frontage and easy access. I also identified something of value. The ground-lease was pre-paid for over a decade into the future. That meant that I could operate this business without paying rent. Or, even more importantly, if I were to find another nursery that needed this location, I could sell the business with pre-paid rent as an asset.

I spent my weekends fixing up the nursery over a few months, dragging my wife and daughter with me. My wife once drove the forklift with me standing on the forks so that I could re-hang shades 20 feet in the air. I paid my 7-year-old daughter to water plants. My neighbor came out and worked for ten bucks an hour as well. We brought it back to life and then went about trying to sell it. I found a buyer who paid multiple-six-figures for the business. I split it with my client. In the end, it paid off for me, and once he realized he was also getting six figures out of the deal, I had a friend for life.

Do you see how I got a free business? An overworked entrepreneur was ambivalent and just gave it to me. But what did I do in order to take advantage of this half-smoked cigar?

The nursery was being run poorly. It was neglected. It looked sad. There was one employee. He was neglected. The plants were neglected. Shade cloth was torn and flapping in the wind. The greenhouse was dry and full of dead plants and old equipment. It was sad. It needed some new energy.

You are probably wondering something. If you take over a business with no money down, what do you do if you need to put money into the company? First, if you end up with a free business, and you need some cash, you might be able to get a loan from your local bank against the company. I could have easily obtained a line of credit for $20,000 or more for the nursery. Also, the Small Business Administration ("SBA") offers loans to fund acquisition or capitalization of small businesses.

There are other ways to get capital as well. You can borrow against your IRA or 401k, for example. Or, if you've followed my advice from the previous chapters, you'll have some side gig money you can use to fund your newly acquired business. With a side gig making steady income, you can use that money to fund the initial revitalization of a wounded business like my nursery. In my particular case, the nursery actually had a bank account with some cash on hand. I used that cash to bring the nursery back to life, but I could have invested some of my own and still made a tidy profit.

Wait. You're asking what's up with that. You're wondering how in the world someone handed me a business that had cash in the bank. Yup. Is that a unique thing? Nope. In fact, later in this book you'll see that there was cash in the bank with two other businesses that I purchased. I've taken over three companies and had cash on hand immediately. You will be surprised at the kind of deals you can work out if you get creative and take over a business someone else wants out of.

With the nursery, I gave it some love for just a few months. It looked like a real business when I was done. It no longer looked like an abandoned and neglected plot of land with a tattered greenhouse and a few dead plants. It was a legit business. I then went to market it for sale. Within a month, I had a buyer. After less than six months of ownership, I was already selling the business. I wasn't going to give it away like my client did. No way. I had a valuable asset. I made six figures in six months by fixing up and flipping a company that someone else had kicked to the curb.

At the same time I was selling this little nursery, I discovered that another business was being sold for $40,000. I won't bore you with the backstory, but a property management company in San Diego was for sale. The owner was looking for an exit. He wanted to retire and sail his boat every day. His property management business was in a shambles. It looked and felt a lot like the nursery. It was a sad business being kicked to the curb. A great opportunity for me.

The price was modest, but he wanted all cash. I'm sure I could have negotiated a payment plan, but I had just sold the nursery and thus had the cash to pay for the management business. For me, it was like getting the management business free, because I paid for it with my winnings from the nursery. Even if I hadn't used nursery profits, the business was a steal. The property management business was doing poorly, but it had an asset that the former owner failed to recognize. The company had a book of pre-paid future reservations that more than paid for the whole purchase of the company within just a few months.

Let me explain. The management company had already collected money for future reservations by vacation renters. That money would come to me as the new owner. There were about $200,000 in booked reservations. That meant that the commission earned (and in the bank) was $40,000 (20% of the total reservations booked). Forty thousand dollars was already in the bank and could be transferred out of trust account[20] and into my bank account in the few months after I bought the business.

Do you see? I paid $40,000 for this little property management business. And when I took over, $40,000 was already mine to collect for management fees. That made my purchase free. Thus, even if I didn't have the cash handy, I could have borrowed $40,000 to purchase the business, and then almost immediately paid it back when I took over the company. I could own the business for nothing out of my pocket. It was free. I stole the business. Two bootleg businesses in a row. Both with cash in the bank. Both with unseen value. It isn't a coincidence. It isn't good luck. It's all about whether or not you are willing to get creative and look for opportunity in what others toss to the curb!

Why did the owner of the property management company sell for so cheap? He was tired and ambivalent. He had just sold a valuable beach apartment complex. He was taking a lot of real estate money off the table, and basically retiring. His little property management business was just an afterthought. In order to

---

20 Realtors hold owner money in a trust account until it is time to pay it to the owner, at which time they can withdraw their commission as well. Here, $200,000 in reservation money would be disbursed, 20% going to the property manager, and the rest going to the owners.

sell it properly and maximize his sale price, he would have had to do a lot of work to clean things up. He just didn't want to do it. The company was not run well; it was dysfunctional, and he didn't care. He was done. So he had three choices: shut it down, sell cheap for a cash payment, or sell and let someone "take over" and make payments. Because I had cash from the nursery sale, I could jump in and pay cash and get the best deal. He was happy and so was I. It was a win-win.

Think I'm just lucky? In the examples above, I stole two businesses in different ways, both with ongoing revenue, and both with existing money in the bank. Well, third time's the charm. I did it again. I purchased LetterPOP in 2009 for a mere $6,000. It had revenue that often exceeded $1,000 per month. Based on the revenue, I would make my investment back in six months. But it turned out this business had a bank account with $6,000 in it. The seller signed the deal requiring that I assume any existing bank accounts. I wasn't aware of the cash until after the deal closed. I didn't really mean to steal LetterPOP. I thought I was getting a good deal because I would make back my investment quickly. When it turned out that the full purchase amount was in the bank account, I realized that I would make my full investment back in one day. It would have been a fine deal without cash in the bank. But because the former owners left the merchant account with a positive balance, the business was free.

I can't be the only one who has basically taken over three companies in 10 years that all turned out to be essentially free. What made these work was that I was willing to hustle and look for opportunity in the trash heap. Warren Buffett isn't the only one who finds half-used cigars on the sidewalk. You can do this, too.

Simple Steps: How You Can Find a Business and Buy It For Nothing

You need to find companies with a seller who is motivated. Sometimes this means finding someone ambivalent like the examples above. Sometimes it involves pressure from partners who don't get along. Often financial pressure forces a business sale. Business owners sometimes get into a financial bind, and if their business isn't growing, they would rather move on and do something else rather than fight their way back into the black.

In addition, personal pressure can motivate a seller. Many sellers are facing a personal dilemma in life: divorce, bankruptcy, health issues. There are many reasons why a business owner decides to sell. If you can find the right situation, then you simply have to create a deal that is a win-win. For example, in my first business venture, a landscape company, I started from scratch. But I grew by acquiring another landscape business. The owner of the selling business was not flourishing, and he had been offered a job working for a larger company. He was faced with two choices: shutting his business down or selling it cheap and getting "something" rather than nothing. I bought that business by working for free for one month, and letting him collect the payments from his old customers for the month. He got one month of free income, and I paid for the business with a non-cash currency: a month of my time.

How do you buy a business when you have no money? Steal it! Get creative. Look at your non-cash currencies. Use future cash from the business by asking the seller to carry back a portion of the purchase. Borrow either against the business or against another asset like your home. Look into SBA loans. Talk to your bank about how you can get a credit line after you buy a business, and then you'll be using the business' own assets to borrow operating capital.

Are three examples enough to convince you that you can bootleg a business? There is always an opportunity to steal a business for those who are willing to think — and look — outside-the-box.

I came across all of my deals serendipitously. But you don't have to wait for something to fall in your lap. You can find deals in many places. Businesses are listed for sale on the local real estate multiple listing service, aka "MLS." Ask your local real estate agent to pull those for you, and they can even give you email alerts so that you see new listings of businesses when they become available. Businesses are listed on Craigslist sometimes. Of course, buyer beware! If you are going to poke around in the proverbial business dump, you'll need to be a careful buyer. There are many great online platforms where businesses are listed for sale, including BizBuySell.com, BizBen.com, BizQuest.com, BusinessBroker.net, and DealStream.com. In addition, you can use a business broker to help you find a deal. Local business brokers are easy to find online. They often specialize in either a local region, where they know the market and typically broker physical businesses. Or they specialize in specific types of businesses regardless of the location (such as AppBusinessBrokers.com, which only broker software-based businesses).

Finding a potential business is the first step. It's a lot of work to find a business that you feel is right for your skills and knowledge. But stealing it requires more imagination.

Here are ideas that can help make this happen for you:

Borrow

If you are going to acquire an ongoing business, then you'll probably be able to borrow at least half of the purchase price from a bank or through an SBA-backed loan. SBA loans can be a few hundred thousand dollars, or they can be many millions of dollars. Educate yourself about the options as you explore the businesses you might want to buy.

Make Payments to the Seller over Time

In almost every business sale, the seller will need to take partial payments to sell the business to anyone. Remember, even when a big private equity group purchases a multi-million-dollar company, it includes a seller-carry component. No one pays full price up-front for a business. How much of the purchase price will the seller carry? Often the seller finances half of a purchase. For a dysfunctional business, there's room to negotiate even more. If there are no other buyers, then a seller might finance the entire business. If you have an SBA loan for half of the purchase, maybe the seller will carry a note for the other half of the purchase price.

I once sold a company on a 100% carry-back. I took payments for five years and sold a business to someone with no money down. It helps if you already have a relationship with the seller. For example, you might be able to take over your boss's business with no money down.

Think creatively. How can you convince a seller to let you take over a business and pay over time? Maybe you are the best person for the business. If the seller takes 50% down from someone else, and they default a year later, then the seller is screwed, right? You should convince a business owner that you are the right choice because you are not going to default. If the seller gives you the business and you keep it running, then over time the seller will get the full value, and not risk selling it to someone who might default.

Use Some Currency Other than Cash

Do you offer a service the seller might need? Are you an attorney or CPA? Offer to trade a block of your time for a certain value toward the purchase of the business. See Chapter 11 on cashless currencies.

With my landscape business, I acquired another person's lawn care business by working the accounts for free for one month. In the end, I bought a great business that expanded my own, while paying nothing out of pocket. I used a non-cash currency to make the deal happen, and it paid off big for me. I was totally broke, had no cash and yet two months later, after the acquisition of his accounts, my business was triple the size and profitable.

Consider trading a used car, RV or boat. What about airline miles or timeshare credit? Anything you have that has value can be offered as part of your effort to get a business with as little cash down as possible.

Reward the Seller on Your Success

Ask a seller to bet on your turnaround. If the company is failing anyhow, and you want to pour your energy into it, then offer a minimum price that you pay over time, plus a bonus based on your success. Let's say that you take over a hair or nail salon. The seller wants $30,000. You offer to pay that $30,000 over five years. You can offer to also pay the seller a small percent of the increase in revenue each year as a bonus for taking a chance on you.

In some cases, you can also let the seller stay a partial owner, and receive distributions of profits. You can buy the old owner out a little more each year, so that the owner keeps her share of the profits while you pay her off over time. You can also offer to share a percentage of the gross or net profit for a period of time. Or offer to pay a certain fixed bonus each year based on growth. This may give a seller an incentive to sell to you with no money down and a bigger upside later, rather than selling to someone else, even if that other buyer has cash.

Make Your Purchase Contingent

You can offer to take over an existing business with no money down, and only consummate the purchase if the business succeeds. Take the example of a salon above. You can offer to test the water by taking over the business for a short period of time, and if you don't find it to be a viable business, then bail out. Once you analyze the opportunity, you can determine if it's right for you and make a decision after that. If it's not a good fit, then you are free to walk away, and the original owner still owns the company and can find another buyer. You might find that the company is like the nursery was for me. You might see that you can take over, fix it up and flip it for a hefty profit and then use those funds to purchase another business that is more long-term.

If you are not obligated to consummate the purchase, and you are just testing the waters, you also might get into a business and realize that it needs too much work. You can still bail out. Or you can go back to the seller and say, "I'm sorry, it isn't worth it. But if you'd like me to take over, I'll pay $15,000. It's just too much of a mess." Taking over a messy business is fine, but you should be sure you are getting a great deal on the purchase.

You need to be in the driver's seat. Look for opportunities and think big. You can bootleg into a business, and it will change your life forever.

Get Creative!

I've given you four examples of cashless business purchases in this chapter from my own experience. My deals aren't special; it is something you can do, too. Don't think that you have to wait years until you "have the money" to buy a business. If you truly want to be self-employed, then you can own a business, and you can do it now. Get creative and be resourceful, and start looking for opportunities!

Due Diligence

Earlier I said "buyer-beware" when looking at businesses for sale on Craigslist. Let me take a moment to say that the old saying *caveat emptor* (buyer-beware) applies to all business investments. If you are going to acquire a business, you will need to do your due diligence. Due diligence is a legal term that is worth understanding. The definition is:

- reasonable steps taken by a person in order to satisfy a legal requirement, especially in buying or selling something.

- a comprehensive appraisal of a business undertaken by a prospective buyer, especially to establish its assets and liabilities and evaluate its commercial potential.

Owning a business isn't like snapping your fingers and making money appear. You need to learn about how business works, and that will help you know what kind of investigation to do when you are looking at a company you might acquire. If you have never owned a business, that doesn't mean you need an MBA. In fact, most successful entrepreneurs don't have any formal training. They've learned what they know from the school of hard knocks, and they are avid readers of books about business. I'm working on a book about how to own and operate a business, but until that's done you should dig into as many business books as you can make time for. I have a list of my favorites in the next chapter.

Forget About Nifty Ideas and Focus on the Money

Once you have gained some knowledge of business, then you'll have some tools for evaluating whether a business is a good deal, or if it's a death trap that may have already brought down the last owner and is likely to ensnare you as well. I can't list every single pitfall here, but I can give you one fundamental thing to consider when you are buying a business. Forget about nifty ideas and focus on the money.

Good ideas don't make good businesses. This speaks to a great American entrepreneurial myth. You don't need a creative idea. You need a business that is generating cash. Focus your due diligence on the cash. Where is it coming from? Where is it going? Can you make more by increasing price? Can you make more by growing the revenue through better marketing, or simply by working harder? Often, businesses that are kicked to the curb are the result of owner neglect. They languish in the hands of someone who is burned out, ambivalent, or even lazy. Once you evaluate the income, then investigate the expenses. Where is the money going? Is there anything you can do to lower costs? Are there costs that seem suspiciously low? If so, then you can ask questions, and those questions should lead you to clear answers. If they do not, then run for the hills! Keep looking until you find a business that survives your due diligence.

What are you hoping for when you conduct your due diligence? You are hoping to get a clear sign that this deal is not worth the risk … or, a clear sign that it is. Take the warning signs seriously and don't get suckered into something that'll waste your time and money. There are good deals to be found. When do you know that the deal is good? You should be able to identify something about the business that gives you confidence that you can increase revenue and decrease expenses. Other great signs would be: valuable inventory that exceeds the price you are paying for the business; cash that comes with the business; unpaid accounts receivable that are clearly likely to be paid after the purchase; earned revenue that comes with the business; something that has a high barrier to entry for competitors (patents, trademarks or content that is unique, for example); long-standing customer relationships; and revenue that is not overly concentrated in one or two customers.

Do as much due diligence as you feel is necessary for the risk. With LetterPOP, I didn't do any. But my risk was low. If it flopped, I'd be out $6,000 and I could afford that loss. But what if the business had cost $60,000 or $600,000? The greater the cost, the more you are putting at risk — and the deeper your due diligence should go as a result.

Chapter Seven:
Bootstrapping a Business

In the last chapter we talked about how to bootleg a business: how to take over an existing business. If you don't have much money, then that's a great way to steal a business that's already going, and then grow it into something awesome. However, taking over an existing company comes with inherent legacy problems created by the old owner. It often means friction and confrontation. It can mean dealing with old creditors, partners, employees and vendors. If you don't have the stomach for those types of messes, then you may want to just start from scratch.

Instead of bootlegging a business, you may need to bootstrap one.

What does it mean to "bootstrap" a business? The phrase comes from the expression "pulling yourself up by your own bootstraps." It's an old saying that is somewhat contradictory. Picture someone pulling themselves up in the air by grabbing their bootstraps and pulling up. It's a funny mental picture. You really can't do it. That's how it feels to start something from scratch without much help or without much money. The "bootstraps" euphemism means doing something without anyone else's help. In business, we use the term to describe starting a company with little money, and running it lean so that your business grows with its own income.

To bootstrap a business, you will be entirely reliant on the resources you have at your disposal. You will not have an investor. You will not have a big budget. You will not have a lot of cash available. Everything you do must be done for free or very cheap. There is nothing wrong with starting a business by virtue of your bootstraps. In fact, it might be the best way to start your first business for one very good reason: no investors. Let me explain.

Many new entrepreneurs want to launch a company by securing venture capital, or a large investment from a professional investor. Every week on TV, people go on Shark Tank to ask the "sharks" to fund their venture. Likewise, every week, new startups approach investment banks, venture capitalists, private equity, and angel investors for money to help launch a company.

It can seem quite appealing to get money from the sharks, or from investors, and get your idea off the ground without any financial stress. Indeed, being a "funded startup" has many advantages. You can immediately hire talented people. You can afford office space. You can engage contractors to build your software, and pay for travel and other business expenses.

However, even with these wonderful advantages, taking invest-ment is not necessarily the best route for first-time entrepre-neurs. First, it is statistically unlikely that you will raise any money this way. In 2013, fewer than 6,000 existing companies globally received "venture"-based funds. There were 3,480 ven-ture capital rounds in 2013. But since funding can occur in mul-tiple rounds to the same company, far fewer than 3,480 compa-nies were actually funded by venture capital.[21]

But wait. The window of opportunity narrows even further: Of those 3,480 rounds of venture funding, most were not directed at startups (meaning new businesses). One group claims that VCs fund only 400 to 600 seed or startup companies per year in America. Most of the venture capital rounds went to existing companies with revenue. With a million companies vying for in-vestors, the odds of getting venture funded are low; you would need to be one of those 400 to 600 early-stage companies that successfully land a venture fund investor.

What about angel investors? Maybe you've heard about investors referred to as "angels." Angels are wealthy individuals willing to make small investments in startups. For example, retired entre-preneurs who want to stay active in the startup world will invest $50,000 to $500,000 in startups. Angels are truly saviors for many startups, and fund far more companies than venture capital firms. However, it is not as many as you might think. One source

---

21 http://www.ey.com/Publication/vwLUAssets/Global_venture_capi-tal_insights_and_trends_2014/$FILE/EY_Global_VC_in-sights_and_trends_report_2014.pdf

says that angel investors fund about 16,000 seed and startup companies per year.[22] Thus, between angel investors and venture capital, about 16,600 startups are funded per year.

That is certainly a lot of angel money flowing into new ventures. However, consider the number of entrepreneurs vying for that money. In the U.S., there are over 500,000 new ventures per month.[23] If we assume that only 15% of the new companies formed are looking for capital, that's one million startups vying for 16,600 investment rounds.

Thus, you have about a 1.5% chance of getting angel funding. Of those who successfully raise investment capital, most are companies founded by someone who has already succeeded in business. Investors are wary about investing in a company run by an untested entrepreneur. They want a track record of success. If you are starting your first venture, then you must be realistic about the opportunities for raising angel and venture funds.

You can see that your odds of raising money from investors are ridiculously slim.

Even if you successfully raise enough money to get your company started, your odds of making millions of dollars are still slim. Once you have secured venture capital financing, your only chance at a substantial exit will either be an IPO (initial public

---

22 http://www.angelblog.net/Angels_Finance_27_Times_More_Startups_Than_VCs.html
See also, Scott Shane, Fool's Gold.
23 http://money.cnn.com/2011/03/07/smallbusiness/new_business_starts/

offering) or an acquisition by a large company or private equity group. Of the companies that successfully raise capital from the venture community, most do not achieve a big sale, and only a few go public.

There's another reason that you should avoid trying to raise money from investors. The process of finding investors is extremely time-consuming. Many entrepreneurs spend their full-time energy just pitching investors. They can't spend much time on the business when they are traveling around looking for investors. A full-time CEO can take an entire year just to raise $250,000 to $500,000. Meanwhile, the company itself needs leadership, time and money.

Bringing investors into a company is expensive. The legal documents alone can be $4,000 to $30,000. You might be able to launch an entire business for the amount of money you would spend on legal and consulting fees.

And investors bring conflict. Investors are humans, and humans (as we all know) can be mean people. When you have a company with mean-spirited investors, you have a big risk that there will be internal conflict. When there is conflict, companies fail. Many of the company failures I have witnessed come from debilitating internal strife. If you own the entire business, you never have to deal with the conflict that comes with investors.

Finally, you don't want to squander your network of potential investors on a bad idea. You only get one shot with an investor. Make sure it's worthwhile. Make it something you have tested and proven to be worth their money. If you bring an investor into your business and succeed, you'll have an investor for life. If you bring an investor into a hair-brained scheme or a business that flails or flops, you'll lose that relationship forever, and of course never get another dime from that investor. Save your potential investors for a future venture with better odds of succeeding.

Bootstrap first; get your company launched and functional. Then, when you approach investors you'll have a better pitch. More importantly, if you wait until you have an operational business, you'll be bringing their money into something that is less experimental. It will no longer just be an idea, and there will be less risk they'll have to contemplate. You'll also diminish your own risk of ruining your relationship with the investor by losing their money.

If you've never started a business before, you should be cautious about taking investment from anyone. You should also be cautious about investing too much of your own capital. You will be your own biggest investor, and you should be very wise about your investment. This does not mean that you should not go into business! It just means you should take it slow and be smart. It's your time and your money, don't throw it away.

This isn't a book about how to start a business. There are plenty of those already. This book is about how to break free from the system and get freedom. You won't get that freedom by trying to raise venture capital to help you launch a business. In fact, running an angel-funded startup might be more burdensome than you think. The Opt Out life is about finding your freedom. You get to live the Opt Out life by owning a business you own entirely, not one that has investors.

How to Bootstrap

I've told you why you need to bootstrap your business: you don't want investors. But, how can you launch a company if you don't have much money? You use your bootstraps! You launch a company with less, rather than more. You do only what is necessary to get the business up and running, to prove that your business idea is valid. If you don't need an office, then don't lease an office. If you don't need staff, then don't hire anyone. If you can function with your old computer, then don't buy a new one. Keep everything as lean as possible.

While bootstrapping has been a theme of startup culture for decades, it was a more recent book that articulated a pathway to bootstrapping a business. Lean Startup, by Eric Ries[24] sets forth several principles that have now been widely embraced by entrepreneurs. One of them is the idea that the first phase of any startup is to develop a minimum viable product (or, "MVP") before taking the company to the next step. Getting your business up and running with an MVP does not require a million-dollar investor.

The first step in bootstrapping is to build a plan you can execute with very little cash. Rather than building a business plan that

---

24 The Lean Startup, Eric Ries (2011)

requires a million dollars, staff, and a fully developed product, start with an MVP, and a team of one or two. Hire a part-time developer, or use contractors on Upwork.com for the first iteration of your product. Let me give you a personal example.

Back in 2005, I saw the need for a way to provide a means for people to incorporate their business entity online. I scoured the market for businesses that offered "online incorporation" services. I found a few. But none were easy to use. None of the services were really doing it well. None offered trademark or copyright filing. Now, the market is huge for this type of service. There are six million new incorporations per year, and most incorporations are done by business owners like you and me, many of whom could use an online service rather than an attorney. I could have developed a plan to launch a massive business, raised millions of dollars, and built a team to launch a full-scale online incorporation service. But, there was simply too much risk. The industry was fragmented. There were a few large companies who offered services to consumers, but they were doing it badly. What if these existing companies suddenly did it well? They could eat my lunch. What if a new player entered the market with greater resources? I'd get my ass kicked.

So, with just a few thousand dollars of my own, I decided to bootstrap the business and launch a small-scale operation (the minimum viable product, or MVP). I hired a software development company in India through eLance (now part of Upwork). I built FileOnline.biz with just a few thousand dollars, and launched within four months. I hired only one part-time staff person. I paid for ads in some business magazines and a single in-flight magazine. I invested $3,000 to develop the website, including a very sophisticated management system. Then I invested about $15,000 into advertising and operational costs. By the third month of business, I had earned my entire investment back. My little experiment was working. I bootstrapped a company, built the MVP, and didn't have to recruit any investors for help.

But something happened after my first few months of successful operations. The price for online ads started going from 50 cents to $2, and then up to $5 per click. That meant my advertising costs went up ten-fold within a few short months. Then I started seeing television ads for a company called LegalZoom that had launched a massive version of the very same business as my FileOnline.biz. Guess whose business got clobbered? Yes, mine did. I could not compete with their ability to pay $5/click for ads. LegalZoom had a massive budget and they were buying market share. They dominated television ads, web ads, affiliate programs and more.

At this point, I had three choices: shut it down, raise money and compete with the big boys, or keep going at a slow rate. I chose to shut it down. The customer acquisition costs were going up so fast that it was no longer viable for me to compete for new customers. Going big was clearly an option. In fact, just because there is a large competitor that is dominating the market, does not mean that someone like me should run and hide. A big company that is succeeding is proof that there is a market! I very well could have determined to dig in deeper, raise money from investors, and compete. However, I had other business ventures already in my portfolio, so I decided to shut down FileOnline.biz. I had made back my investment, and did not want to put more at risk. Because I had bootstrapped this little venture, I was able to make this decision without losing my shirt. In fact, I didn't lose anything.

What if my business was not a bootstrapped venture, but one backed by investors? Instead of starting it with $20,000 of my own money, I could have hired staff, leased an office, engaged an advertising agency, and used $500,000 of investment to get to the same place. The result would have been catastrophic! When LegalZoom hit the market, my business would have still faced the same challenges, but now it would have the added pressure of investors expecting a return on their investment. I would have then needed to seek additional investment and go head-to-head with the big players in that market.

You probably don't have hundreds of thousands of dollars to launch your startup. You might be starting your first venture with $1,500 in savings, a little of your side gig income, and a small loan from your uncle. If you fail, it will be miserable, but it won't be the end of the world. And you'll be able to recover from that failure and launch again using the same principles. If you start a business with your bootstraps, you'll be able to use those same bootstraps again. If you try to launch a business with investor money, you'll burn your bridges and may not get a second chance.

You can see that starting a business has a major financial risk. You'll bootstrap your business to diminish that risk. You'll want to put very little money at risk, and then if the venture fails, you can easily recover and try again.

Money isn't the only thing you put at risk when you start a business. You'll be using other resources as well, such as your time.

Time is a precious and valuable commodity. Your time is your largest investment when you launch a business. You'll want to use it wisely. Let's take FileOnline.biz as an example of how to invest your time wisely. I launched that business with less than ten hours per week of my time, over the span of a few months. I was risking very little in terms of the time invested. When it flopped, I didn't lose that much in the value of my time. That's just as important as the fact that I was not putting very much money into the venture.

You may not yet understand the value of your time. If you are going to be self-employed, you should come to terms with the fact that your time is money: It is worth something. You can choose what to do with your time, and if you choose wisely, you'll make money with your time. If you don't use your time wisely, then you'll lose money with your time.

What did I lose when my little venture failed? I lost about 100 hours of my time. That's not cheap by any means. My time in 2005 may have been worth $200 per hour. That's $20,000 in my valuable time. But it was a small investment compared to other things I could have done with my time. For example, what if instead of trying to bootstrap a company, I had raised venture capital? I would have spent 8 to 12 hours per day raising capital for a year. I would also have spent long days working with a team of employees to launch the venture. By the time I would have launched a fully-venture-funded version of FileOnline.biz, I would logged at least 2,000 hours into it. That would be $400,000 in my time. If the venture failed, rather than merely losing the value of $20,000 in time, I would have lost nearly a half-million dollars in my time.

Learn to respect that your time has value, and consider it an investment when you are putting it to use in business. It can be used to make money. Even if your time is not worth $200 per hour, it still has value. In addition, your time has an additional value in what we call "opportunity value." What else could you do with your time that could produce a higher value? I was cautious with the amount of time I invested into this venture. That way, I only lost the value of 100 hours as well as the opportunities that I could have created with those 100 hours. Clearly, the opportunity cost of 2,000 hours compared to 100 hours is massive. Who knows what could have been if I hadn't lost that much opportunity value?

This bootstrapping thing might seem scary. How can you start a business with nothing?

Consider what you can start cheap. How cheap? Well, Chris Guillebeau, author of The $100 Startup, says you can launch a startup for, you guessed it, $100.[25] I've personally launched businesses on very small budgets, but none quite as low as that. However, Guillebeau offers a compelling case for getting into business with very little money.

When I started my landscape company as a twenty-year-old entrepreneur, I didn't even have a work truck. I used my Volkswagen Golf to carry a cheap lawnmower and cheap used landscape equipment. In a matter of one year, that business was employing several people, and had two trucks, four sets of equipment, and was paying my way through college. A few years later, I sold the company and made a fair sum, for a 23-year-old.

You can start many businesses with very little cash, including service businesses such as lawn care and pool cleaning. Many of today's startups are web-based. With an internet business, you don't even need to buy a lawnmower or pool cleaning equipment. Websites can be built from scratch for free, and sophisticated mobile apps can be built for a few thousand dollars even if you are not a programmer.

I personally know of more than a dozen mobile applications that have been created for under $4,000 each. Of course, if you are willing to learn to program, you can launch a web or mobile application with almost no cash investment. One programmer I know launched a mobile application for tracking your weight. It

---

25 The $100 Startup, Chris Guillebeau (2012)
http://www.amazon.com/The-100-Startup-Reinvent-Living/dp/0307951529

was a simple app that he sold on the Android marketplace for three bucks. That one app paid him over $2,000 per month for many years. His cost? About six weeks of his time, and no cash. He didn't advertise. He didn't spend a dime.

Blogs are another way of starting a business from scratch with no money out of pocket. Starting a blog requires no cash up front. If your content is valuable, then you'll make money. A blog can start as a side gig, and can grow into a real business. If you create unique content that brings regular traffic to your blog, then you can make money by using Google Adsense to run ads on your blog. In addition, if your blog has quality content, you might be able to make money by charging people a fee to post their content on your blog. There are many companies that will pay bloggers to put "sponsored" content on their blogs so that the sponsor can gain credibility from the blog. You get paid to post content, and the sponsor gets increased traffic, and also gets higher rank in the search engines because of the sponsored post that they run on your blog.

Think through the side gig examples I've provided in the previous chapters. Most of those required no cash up front. Your side gig can turn into a business. Even if it doesn't, you can use the funds from your side gig to finance your business. If you use your side gig income to finance your business, then your business is being launched for free because the funds are coming from a side gig that cost you nothing to start. That's why starting a side gig first gives you more options for choosing a business. You can weigh the options once your side gig is flourishing. If it has the potential to grow into a full business, then you let it evolve. If not, then you keep it going while you work on starting a business from scratch, and the side gig helps fund it.

Here are some low-cost strategies for starting a business from scratch:

- Outsource development of websites and software applications

  o Use Upwork or some other outsource platform to use developers in the U.S., as well as overseas workers from around the world.

- Start with a simple product and test it to see if it works before you order large volumes

  o Have samples of your product made, and promote the product to see if people like it. Don't spend thousands of dollars on a new product idea before you test it. Sell 3D printed samples in the beginning even if you lose money. If it goes well, you'll make it back once you can sell higher volumes. You can pay third-party services like Shape-Ways.com to create your prototype and samples.

- Fake it

  o Tim Ferriss (have I mentioned Mr. Ferriss?) advocates the idea of offering a product for sale just to see if it works, even before you're able to deliver the product. If it sells, then you can start producing your product. If it doesn't, then cancel the orders, refund the payments and apologize profusely.

- Start with the simplest set of equipment you really need

  o Want to have a pool cleaning service? Don't buy a truck and all the equipment. Buy only what you need. Borrow and rent equipment. When you get customers, you can then acquire the rest.

- Skip the office

  o Most people perceive that they need an office. You don't. Start with a postal box, or an executive suite until you need space. You may never need office space.

- Skip the staff

  o You can hire part-time contractors if you aren't ready to hire employees. Don't rush to create a team of people before you are ready to have dependents. You can hire later, and maybe even hire your independent contractors. Start small.

- Outsource your bookkeeping

  o Good bookkeeping is essential. You can pay under $100 per month in some cases, and start your venture with clean financials. This will save money and headaches later when you go to file taxes.

- Give incentives tied to success

  o Many entrepreneurs start a venture and

then quickly offer stock to employees and contractors. Be careful not to give away stock in your company. In most cases, employees don't understand or value stock. The better option is to offer bonuses and incentives for success, rather than giving away equity in your company.

- Collaborate

  o Find someone who is doing a complementary business and try to collaborate with them. Piggyback on their success. Share resources. Reciprocate revenue, and pay each other for referrals. Collaboration is a great way to bootstrap.

- Keep going back to your MVP (Minimum Viable Product): keep it simple until you prove that your business idea is working

  o Don't pay to automate something if you can do it manually in the beginning. For example, your software might need to process transactions manually in the beginning; you can wait until there's steady revenue before you incur the cost of making transactions automatic.

You might be wondering whether you are the right person to start a business. It's easy for me to tell you that the best way to get ahead is to own your own business — I wrote a book on it, after all. The reality, however, is that owning a business isn't for everyone. Many are just not cut out for owning a business, and certainly aren't equipped for starting one from scratch.

The good news is that anyone can learn. However, you might find the very idea of running a business to be paralyzing. I have a very good friend who spent a few months working through this question. She had it in her mind to start a business. As she worked through the early planning stages, she had panic attacks. She ultimately realized she was far better off to keep working in her career than to run a business. That has not prevented her from doing side gigs! She's done everything else in this book, but owning a business isn't for her.

You may not know if you are naturally business savvy until you start. If that's you, then start slow and ask a lot of questions. Learn everything you can along the way. You'll find mentors all around you once you get started. Your accountant will be a rich source of advice, as will your business attorney. You can join associations that will function to educate you and expand your network.

Maybe owning a business doesn't scare you, but you want to have a system in place that helps ensure success. That's perfectly okay! Franchises might be a good idea for those who want to own a business but don't want to deal with buying a broken business, or don't want to start from scratch. There are entire trade shows dedicated to franchise opportunities, such as Franchise Expo, which operates regional shows around the country. There are franchise brokers who can help you scout deals, and also provide analysis of the potential deals that come your way. Take your time, perform your due diligence, and be sure you are comfortable with your choice.

I've said that most businesses fail in the first few years. That's good news for you when it comes to buying a broken business. It's also foreboding because your business might fail as well. Many good people are dashed on the rocks of failed entrepreneurship. I have two things to say about that. First, you can hedge against failure with knowledge. Be humble and learn. You don't know everything and you never will. It takes time to get good at business. Give yourself the room to figure it out. Second, you might fail … and that's perfectly okay. Every great entrepreneur has experienced failure on some level. I've described shutting down my own businesses in these pages. It's okay to fail, as long as you learn and are able to go at it again. Don't let the fear of failure prevent you from becoming an entrepreneur. But do your best to insure against failure with knowledge and careful planning.

As I said earlier, this book isn't intended to be your complete guide to starting a business, but to present a framework to opt out and live the good life. One component is owning a business. However, owning a business may require skills or knowledge you don't have. This book focuses on the philosophy. When it comes to actually doing business, you'll need to learn more.

There are a host of video courses that are available to help you become an entrepreneur. Consider the hundreds of videos on Linkedin Learning, where you can learn very specific business skills (like my courses on business and intellectual property law26), as well as leadership27, entrepreneurship[28], and more.

Also, build your library and start reading! Here's a list of some excellent books that every entrepreneur should read.

Start Your Own Business, Sixth Edition: The Only Startup Book You'll Ever Need by The Staff of Entrepreneur Media.[29]

Small Time Operator: How to Start Your Own Business, Keep Your Books, Pay Your Taxes, and Stay Out of Trouble by Bernard B. Kamoroff C.P.A.[30]

The $100 Startup: Reinvent the Way You Make a Living, Do What You Love, and Create a New Future by Chris Guillebeau.[31]

The Lean Startup: How Today's Entrepreneurs Use Continuous Innovation to Create Radically Successful Businesses by Eric Ries.[32]

---

26 https://www.linkedin.com/learning/search?keywords=dana%20robinson

27 https://www.linkedin.com/learning/search?keywords=leadership%20+%20management&trk=featured_skill

28 https://www.linkedin.com/learning/search?keywords=entrepreneurship

29 https://www.amazon.com/s/ref=dp_by-line_sr_book_1?ie=UTF8&text=The+Staff+of+Entrepreneur+Media&search-alias=books&field-author=The+Staff+of+Entrepreneur+Media&sort=relevancerank

30 https://www.amazon.com/s/ref=dp_by-line_sr_book_1?ie=UTF8&text=Bernard+B.+Kamoroff+C.P.A.&search-alias=books&field-author=Bernard+B.+Kamoroff+C.P.A.&sort=relevancerank

31 https://www.amazon.com/Chris-Guillebeau/e/B003G218QO/

32 https://www.amazon.com/Eric-Ries/e/B004VIDMR0/

The Startup Owner's Manual: The Step-By-Step Guide for Building a Great Company Steve Blank by Bob Dorf.[33]

Rich Dad Poor Dad: What The Rich Teach Their Kids About Money That the Poor and Middle Class Do Not! by Robert T. Kiyosaki.[34]

Think and Grow Rich by Napoleon Hill.[35]

The Richest Man in Babylon byGeorge S. Clason.[36]

The Millionaire Next Door: The Surprising Secrets of America's Wealthy by Thomas J. Stanley, William D. Danko.[37]

The 4-Hour Workweek: Escape 9-5, Live Anywhere, and Join the New Rich by Timothy Ferriss.[38]

Zero to One: Notes on Startups, or How to Build the Future by Peter Thiel, Blake Masters.[39]

Ultimately, getting the Opt Out life means working for yourself and not for The Man. Bootleg a business or bootstrap one.

When you start a business by bootstrapping, rather than by using someone else's money, you'll naturally make smarter choices. Using your own resources forces you to be practical, and smarter, with how you use your money. When you have someone else's

---

33 https://www.amazon.com/Steve-Blank/e/B002IBT21M/
34 https://www.amazon.com/Robert-T.-Kiyosaki/e/B001H6GV90/
35 https://www.amazon.com/Napoleon-Hill/e/B000APAMYE/
36 https://www.amazon.com/George-S.-Clason/e/B000APM8VY/
37 https://www.amazon.com/Thomas-J.-Stanley/e/B000APC2MY/
38 https://www.amazon.com/Timothy-Ferriss/e/B001ILKBW2/
39 https://www.amazon.com/Peter-Thiel/e/B00J0W47NA/

money, it can be easy to make decisions that are not as grounded in reality. I'm not saying you would be sloppy with someone else's money. Wait, yes, I am saying that you would be sloppy with someone else's money. I know of a really smart guy, an attorney and Rhodes Scholar, who was part of a venture-funded startup that spent $40,000 in legal fees in the first year. The business had a lawyer on staff! It didn't need to spend $40,000 on other lawyers! For that $40,000, the business filed a pending patent (that never issued); filed a few trademarks; incorporated; wrote a stock option plan, and the legal documents for its fundraising. It was just a wasteful use of funds. They didn't need that much legal work. It was sloppy to blow that money on attorneys. Trust me, I'm a lawyer. Using your own resources forces you to use discipline with your money.

But where is that money going to come from?

If you follow my advice in this book, you'll reinvent your lifestyle. You'll be living a smart, "scavenger" life, and your income will be the best it's been. You'll have a little side gig generating extra income. You'll have lower expenses because you'll have found creative ways to reduce your cost of living, like the many examples found throughout this book. If you have put yourself in that position, then you are ready to take a bit of a risk and consider starting or buying a business.

Again, don't be afraid to skip this whole entrepreneurship thing! At the end of the day, be sure you want to be in business before you start one! Maybe you don't need a business after all. A business requires a lot of work. It may take all your free time for many years. If what you want to do is travel, or have an easy life, then don't start a business. You only need the side gig. Stop there, and go live. Dance in Spain. Dine in Paris. Ride motorbikes across Russia. Climb a mountain. Meditate in the rice fields of Bali. Start a band. Write music or poetry or a novel. Learn seven languages. You can live an amazing life without ever starting a business. You can apply my other methods and end up with more freedom and money than you imagined, while never being tied down to a business.

Chapter Eight:
Real Estate the Scavenger Way

Real estate creates passive income that goes up with the value of currency: It is inflation-proof. Remember Chapter 3 and what happened to my great-grandfather's wealth? It went down in value with rising inflation. My grandmother never invested in real estate. My grandmother in 1937 could have used $100,000 of her inheritance to buy 20 single family homes at $5,000 each. Those 20 houses would be worth $500,000 each today. That's $10 million. She still could have used her remaining $200,000 in cash to live the lush life. If she had put all $300,000 of her cash into buying income property, that would have led to an estate worth $30 million today. And she would have lived a far better life throughout the years because she would have had increasing income from the rent on those properties (and I would have inherited my share of a $30 million estate!).

While is easy to see how devastating inflation is over many decades, we can even see it in our own lifetime. When I rented my first apartment in 1990, it cost $300 per month. That same unit now rents for $2,500. In the year 2000, weekly rent for an ocean-front vacation condo was $800 per week. I own that same condo today, and it rents for $3,800 per week. Rental income grows with inflation. That is why it is one of the most essential elements of the Opt Out life.

Real estate is one of the key income pillars for escaping moderate poverty. I've known dozens of millionaires. Every single one of them say that real estate was the key to building their wealth. When it comes to your rise out of moderate American poverty, real estate presents the primary way to leapfrog ahead.

Do you own your home? Okay, that's great. But that's not a real estate investment.

Most Americans have the mistaken belief that owning a home is the same as having an investment in real estate. Your home is not an investment. It is a liability. Your home costs you something. Even if you own your home cash with no mortgage, you have recurring expenses tied to the property. You must earn other money to pay your housing expenses. If you have a mortgage, then your expenses are that much higher. It costs you money, rather than generating income. That means your home is a lia-bility and not an asset. In the next chapter, I'll show you how to make your home an asset, but for purposes of this chapter, it's important to understand that owning real estate means owning income property and not just owning the house you live in.

I'm not saying that you should not own a home. Owning a residence is a reasonable means of preparing for retirement. In California, where our property taxes are locked-in at our purchase price, owning a home is an even wiser, long-term financial play than in other states. But, just because owning a home is a wise use of financial resources, it should not be considered a real estate investment.

For purposes of the Opt Out life, we will focus on real estate which generates income that offsets the cost of ownership, generates excess cash flow, and also appreciates with time. Real estate also provides a unique opportunity to "shift" some of what you would otherwise pay in taxes through depreciation. I'll talk more about depreciation below, and again in Chapter 10.

What about your residence? When it comes to creating financial independence, you should live in a home that you can afford easily. Live in it and enjoy it and pay it down over time. Don't get an interest-only loan. Pay your house off! Don't buy a bigger house as your income rises. Make your house an affordable comfortable environment that is a safety net, not a burden. Or, just rent! You don't need to own your home to achieve financial independence. I don't own mine. You'll see that I've been able to live an incredible lifestyle, living in multimillion-dollar oceanfront homes for almost nothing. While I don't own my residence, I do own rental properties. Real estate has been a key to my financial independence.

Real Estate Investing

The best real estate for a beginner is residential rental property. A residential rental property is a single-family house or a small complex with two, three or four units. Rental properties with five or more units are referred to as "multi-family rental properties." I've owned single-family and four-plex properties, as well as multi-family complexes. Both types of income property can be great investments. But owning smaller properties is the best place to begin.

I've owned apartment complexes. That might be where you eventually invest. But for purposes of this book, I'm not prescribing commercial or multi-family real estate. One reason is that it's really hard to manage dozens (or hundreds) of units. Another reason that you don't need to own apartment complexes is that you only really need to own a few properties in order to get the maximum benefit of owning real estate. In most cases, you probably only need to own two or three houses, or a couple of small duplex or triplex properties.

Let me start with the truth about rental property: It's a total pain in the ass. Especially when you own larger apartment complexes. Those who own real estate can attest to the fact that it will interrupt the most important and intimate moments of your life. One great example was when I was out with friends celebrating my birthday, eating the most amazing *dulce de leche* cake at San Diego's famed Extraordinary Desserts. My phone rang. It was my sister, who managed almost 100 units of apartments in Phoenix for me.

"Hi Dana. I'm so sorry to bother you on your birthday. I tried to avoid it. But, I have a problem."

"Hey sis. No worries. It comes with the territory. What's the problem?" I said.

"Well, there was a leak. I had to get a plumber out here to find it. He's dug a five-by-five hole in your parking lot, and he found the source. It's several feet down. He can fix it. But we don't have an account with him. He needs your credit card before he'll finish the work."

"Ugh," I moaned, stepping away from the table. "How much does he need?" I was thinking this would be expensive, like at least 500 bucks.

She said, "Sit down if you aren't already." I sat.

"Five thousand dollars," she said quietly. I gasped.

Nice birthday present, right? Five grand in one swipe! That was the icing on my dulce de leche birthday cake!

I breathed a deep breath, and said, "Okay, here it is."

Unfortunately, it is not uncommon to have this type of problem when you own apartment complexes. It isn't just the repair bills. Tenants can be a serious problem. I once owned a building that my assistant nicknamed "Jerry Springer" because the tenants were just those kind of people, with that kind of drama. Imagine learning that a tenant has borrowed the manager's keys to access other apartments so they could steal other tenants' booze. True story. How about a hailstorm that takes out a section of your roof in less than an hour? On-site maintenance staff who steal from you, contractors who rip you off, and tenants who use your apartment as a meth lab are all the risks you take in owning real estate.

Yes, property ownership is full of hassles and unpleasant surprises, but it is one of the keys to building wealth. Whether you are a seasoned investor, or trying to climb your way out of the rat race, you should invest in real estate despite these hazards.

The main advantages to owning real estate are as follows:

1. You can finance the property and use the rental income to pay the mortgage. You can't do that with stock, bonds or most other investments.

2. You don't need to pay in full when you buy a rental property. This allows you to control an asset that is worth a lot more than you have in cash.

3. The income goes up with inflation, while your mortgage stays the same. Over time, that means rent goes up while your expenses remain low. When you pay the property off, the income is part of your retirement, and continues to rise with inflation.

4. The value of the property goes up with inflation and thus, as an asset it insulates you against inflation.

5. You get a small, but meaningful, passive loss that translates to annual savings on your taxes.

6. If you leave property to your heirs, they don't pay taxes on the appreciation during your life (a principle called stepped-up-basis).

7. If you move into a rental property and make it your primary home for two years, when you sell it you don't pay taxes on the first $250,000 in gains ($500,000 for a married couple).

I'm going to give you the $25,000 tax reason to own some real estate. You don't need to own entire apartment buildings to take advantage of an important tax write-off worth $25,000 per year. The rich have many tax loopholes. You and I only have a few. One of them is the ability to take a loss of up to $25,000 on real estate.

It is this $25,000 loophole that makes it extra important to own real estate. It also is the reason that you don't need to own too much real estate. My prescription is to own "just enough" real estate to take advantage of the maximum depreciation, while getting the benefits of appreciation, and a hedge against inflation. Let me explain.

When you own rental property, you own two components of real estate: the land and the building(s). The land theoretically appreciates over time. Appreciation can come from buying land that goes up in value as the area becomes denser. It can also "appreciate" by maintaining its value while the value of the dollar goes down. Remember, our little enemy inflation from Chapter 3? It's inevitable.

Real estate tends to hold its "core" value while the dollar's buying power drops over time. So even if there is no significant increase in the value of the property, you can sell it for more later because of inflation. In addition, inflation will drive up the rental income that you charge your tenants. If you buy real estate wisely, you will get small increases in rental income, an increase in real value, and also an increase in value from inflation.

But appreciation and hedging inflation are not the only reasons to own income property. You get to write off the structures that are on your property because the structures technically depreciate. You write these off over time, even if they are not actually worth less each year. For most properties, the time frame for depreciation is 27 years. This means that you write off 1/27th of the cost of your structures each year.

Here's an example. Assume you acquire a property for $500,000, and the structures are worth $270,000 of the $500,000. You will write off the $270,000 structure as an expense. You write it off over 27 years, taking 1/27th ($10,000) per year deduction on your tax return. That constitutes $10,000 that you can use to offset your other income. If you are in the 28% tax bracket, then this saves you nearly $3,000 in actual cash each year.

You can write off up to $25,000 per year in this type of loss. Thus, using my example above, you could own two properties worth $500,000 each (with structures each worth $270K), and you would get $20,000 in losses. That should net you about $6,000 in actual cash that you would keep rather than pay to the IRS. If your two properties made no actual profit, you would still be

$6,000 per year ahead. If you take that $6,000 per year and put it into your long-term retirement plan starting at 30 years old, by the time you are 63, you will have added $1 million to your retirement. In addition, you will have paid off your two properties and they will have appreciated to be worth far more than the original $500,000 each. Over time, the income will increase on your properties, making you richer both in current income, and in your total net worth.

I am not a CPA or tax attorney. You need to be sure you follow the law and use a great CPA to help you understand the tax implications of your investing. Tax laws are in flux, and may change this calculus. Also, when you make investments, use a professional. My projections are based on the CNN Mortgage Calculator.[40]

I hope you can see that you don't need to own hundreds of apartments for real estate to work for you. You need a few residential properties, or a 2 to 4-unit complex. In fact, you can buy 2 to 4-unit apartment complexes with as little as 3.5% down with FHA financing, as long as you live in one of the units when you purchase the property.

Many people think that owning rental property is out of their league. It isn't. You can start with one rental house, or you can go straight to four units. Whatever approach you choose, remember that the goal is to own just enough real estate to take

---

40 http://money.cnn.com/calculator/retirement/retirement-need/

advantage of the passive losses you can write off. In my circumstance, I own one beach condo, and one four-plex. The two properties generate my maximum loss of $25,000, saving me about $8,000 per year that I would otherwise have to pay the government. The properties don't actually lose money, though. The properties generate cash flow, pay down their own mortgages, and save me $8,000 in taxes.

Should you own more properties? This is a personal decision. I advocate owning just enough because I've owned too much! There's a high personal cost to own and manage larger complexes. Managing a few units is something you can do without hiring a professional manager, especially if you buy properties in your own town. You can find your own contractors and ensure that you aren't being ripped off. If you own real estate on a larger scale this is more difficult. Through the years, I've directly managed my properties, and I've used several different management companies. None of them were more profitable than self-management. You'll be much better off if you directly oversee your own properties. Own just enough real estate to take advantage of the tax losses. On the other hand, own only as much as you can manage yourself.

One of the most important pieces of advice about real estate is that you should buy near where you live. I know of many horror stories that involve real estate in faraway places. It can be very tempting to buy an $80,000 rental house in Oklahoma. But if you live in California or New York, you are better off buying near where you live. There are two reasons. One is that you're better able to handle the problems on your own. The other reason is that you will know a good investment in your area; you won't know how to identify a good investment in another state. Don't be enticed by cheap real estate that's hundreds of miles away from you.

Examples of Getting Into Real Estate Cheaply

Let me give you a few examples of how to get into real estate. It doesn't always cost as much as you think. Here are some stories to help illustrate the Opt Out way of getting into real estate. It's not much different than stealing a business or a side gig. You've got to think unconventionally.

Earlier, I talked about a friend who bought a duplex. She battled internal and external forces and family arguments, but in the end she bought a duplex rather than a condo or house. If she had purchased a condo or house, she would be responsible for the entire mortgage. Instead, she bought a duplex. Her purchase price was $660,000, and she used a loan that provided another $90,000 for refurbishing the property. She put only $30,000 down. Her mortgage and property taxes cost $5,500 a month. After renovating the property, she rented the second unit for $2,000 per month. That makes her share of the mortgage just $2,500 a month, which is less than she was paying to rent an apartment in San Diego. The rent on the second unit will go up year after year, and her own cost will stay the same or go down with time. Eventually, she can move out and rent the second unit. The property will then be cash flow-positive, and make her money every month.

And don't forget depreciation. Because she owns real estate that she can depreciate, she's saving about $2,000 a year in actual cash on her tax return. As a homeowner, she can also expense her mortgage interest. Her total annual savings is about $5,000. She also reduced her expenses because her apartment rent was higher than her current monthly cost.

How did she do it? She used an FHA loan that only required 3.5% down. Between her down payment and closing costs, she put down $30,000. As a result, she has a home, a rental unit, and is paying down the mortgage with her tenant's rental payments — not to mention saving thousands of dollars each year in taxes. In addition, once the rehab was complete, the value of the property increased by over two hundred thousand dollars. A year after she finished the rehab, the property was worth about $1 million.

Keep in mind this was a property located in a prime neighborhood. In most cities across the U.S., you can do the same type of deal with far less than $30,000 down. You can use FHA financing with 3.5% down on any condo, house or a property with 2 to 4 units. Consider, for example, a $400,000 four-plex. If you live in one unit, you can buy it with less than $20,000 down. The rent from the other three units might pay the entire mortgage. After you have lived in the property for a year or two, move out and do it all over again.

You may not even need to use FHA for a loan. You might be able to swing the conventional 20% down. When I bought my first rental property, I was looking to buy a beach condo. The price of the condo would exceed the FHA loan limits, and I needed to come up with 20%. I had no savings whatsoever. So I went to work trying to hustle up a solution. My goal was to come up with enough to buy a $330,000 beach condo.

The first step was to find some ways to boost my cash position. I landed a side gig that made me over $10,000, helping a wealthy friend liquidate a house full of furniture. I may as well tell you about the side gig, even though we aren't in the side gig chapter. My wealthy friend had purchased a large oceanfront four-plex. He didn't want to own a four-plex. He wanted to build a mansion. That four-plex was in his way. Not only was the four-plex in his way, but all of the furniture was in his way, too. Four units full of furniture, appliances, décor, linens, beach toys, chairs, and more. One day he told me he was going to see if he could find someone to haul it away for free. He figured he'd probably need to pay someone to come haul it all off. It was used furniture and needed to be removed before the structure could be demolished. My wife jumped in and asked if we could hold a massive garage sale and sell the contents of the four units. She said we would happily split the profit with my millionaire friend. He laughed and said, "You're joking, right?" No, my wife said flatly, and she pressed him for permission to hold the garage sale. He relented. A week or so later, we were hosting a massive four-plex liquidation sale. We hired my parents, my aunt and a friend to help. In a matter of three days, we liquidated the place. We even sold the used countertops to a guy who came with tools and pulled them out. Someone paid us for the recessed lights and removed those, too. In the end, we hauled away a new washer and dryer that we kept for ourselves, and about $12,000 in cash. We paid our helpers, covered some meals and travel, and headed home $10,000 richer. Oh, and my benevolent friend told us to keep his share of the profit.

If you've ever had ten grand in cash dropped in your lap, it's tempting to use it to improve your lifestyle. At the time, I really needed a car. But, my goal was to buy a beach condo, so I kept driving my beat-up Volvo 240 and saved the money. I then received a bonus from my work of $7,000. Again, many people blow their bonus on toys, cars and technology. I kept my bonus in a separate savings account. Now, I had $17,000. I was getting closer to what I needed to buy the condo.

At the time, I lived in a small house that had gone up in value a little. I borrowed $20,000 against my primary residence. That gave me $37,000. Is that enough to get into a $330,000 beach property? Yes. It turned out to be enough. My loan broker found a split loan: a first mortgage of $260,000 and a second mortgage of $33,000. My down payment was $33,000. I bought a beach condo when only a few months earlier I didn't have any cash at all.

That's how I pulled together the resources to get the property. That's your first step. The next step is to be sure you can pay for it once you own it.

The rental income from the beach condo for the first year was about $30,000. This provided enough income to pay the two mortgage payments, and the second mortgage on my primary residence. I also saved a couple thousand dollars each year in taxes. Within a year, I refinanced the property and consolidated the two mortgages at a lower interest rate, and dropped my mortgage payment to about $1,600 a month, making the investment even more profitable. If I still owned that property, it would be making far more income, and still only costing $1,600 every month. In fact, it would be halfway to being paid off. Instead, I chose to sell it when the market went crazy, and made over $300,000 in profit. I used that money to buy other properties, including a million-dollar beach condo that now makes over $80,000 per year in income, and an apartment complex.

Many people perceive that they would need to come up with $70,000 to buy my $330,000 condo (e.g. 20% down). They don't realize that owning real estate is within their grasp. I hustled to earn $10,000, and then used creative borrowing to finance the condo. You can do it too. Don't let your misperceptions hold you back from owning real estate.

I know of a man who bought a three-unit complex in a nice area for $900,000. The total rental income for the three units was $7,500 a month. He used an FHA loan and borrowed the 3.5% down payment from his 401k. His mortgage and expenses were about $6,000 a month. He had positive cash flow of $1,500 per month immediately. He used that income to pay back his 401k for the down payment. He basically got into a million-dollar property without any real cash of his own. He borrowed the small down payment. And he now controls an asset worth almost $1 million.

Over the course of 30 years, the mortgage will be paid down and rent will increase, adding more every year to his income. In addition, depreciation gives him a tax write-off of $16,666 each year for 27 years. He will have saved over $5,000 in taxes every year. That's more than $400 per month that he isn't paying the IRS, and that money goes directly into his pocket.

Rent goes up each year. In 10 years, my buddy will be making $3,000 per month after expenses, his mortgage will be getting paid off, and he'll have that same $400 a month in tax savings. At retirement, when that property is fully paid off, he should be making over $10,000 in net income every month. That's more than most Americans retire on. And it's not his only asset. He owns a business that he'll eventually sell. He has a 401k, and he's invested in other real estate.

This book isn't intended to show you all the ins and outs of real estate investing. There are many great books on the subject. There are two points to take away from this section. First, you need to own just enough rental property. Second, you can do this without being rich.

Rental property needs to be part of your plan to rise from moderate poverty. The impact of rental property on your income, your taxes, and your wealth is striking. Pick up some books on real estate investing and get a hand in the game. Here are a few to get you started:

The Millionaire Real Estate Investor by Gary Keller, Dave Jenks,

Jay Papasan (2005)[41]

The Book on Rental Property Investing: How to Create Wealth and Passive Income Through Smart Buy & Hold Real Estate Investing by Brandon Turner (2015)[42]

Rich Dad Poor Dad: What The Rich Teach Their Kids About Money That the Poor and Middle Class Do Not! by Robert T. Kiyosaki (2011)[43]

What Every Real Estate Investor Needs to Know about Cash Flow... And 36 Other Key Financial Measures by Frank Gallinelli (2003)[44]

Building Wealth One House at a Time, Updated and Expanded, John Schaub (2016)[45]

The Unofficial Guide to Real Estate Investing by Spencer Strauss, Martin Stone (2003)[46]

---

41 https://www.amazon.com/Millionaire-Real-Estate-Investor/dp/0071446370 /

42 https://www.amazon.com/Book-Rental-Property-Investing-Intelligent/dp/099071179X/

43 https://www.amazon.com/Rich-Dad-Poor-Teach-Middle/dp/1612680011/

44 https://www.amazon.com/Every-Estate-Investor-Financial-Measures/dp/0071422579/

45 https://www.amazon.com/Building-Wealth-Updated-Expanded-Second/dp/1259643883/

46 https://www.amazon.com/Unofficial-Guide-Estate-Investing-Guides/dp/0764537091/

The Live-In-It Flippers

At the outset of this chapter, I said that your home is not an investment. It is not an asset. It is a liability. Well, there's one major exception: those crazy couples who buy a house, fix it up while they live in it, and then sell it. Flippers are using a combination of strategies that include two tax loopholes, and their own sweat equity to create wealth very quickly. Because they are living in their investment property, their "home" isn't a liability like it is for you or me. For them, their home is an asset.

How does that work?

These live-in-it-flippers work on the house while they live in it. They do some of the fix-up on their own in the evening and on weekends. They hire and manage sub-contractors to lay carpet, rehab the bathrooms, and redo the landscape. They save thousands by using their sweat and elbow grease. When they sell, they hope to make enough to compensate for their hard work and time that they could have used to make money elsewhere. They work hard and live in a construction zone while they rehab the house. It isn't a job for the faint of heart.

The rehab work increases the value of the property so that they can sell it for more than they paid. It may also go up in value for other reasons. As I've mentioned, sometimes real estate goes up in core value because of increased urbanization. Other times, value goes up from gentrification. Even if the value doesn't go up from these things, the apparent value can go up because of inflation. The buying power of the dollar drops, and makes the property worth more dollars. While the live-in-it-flippers are in the house, they get some increase from all of these modes of appreciation.

The flippers are also looking to take advantage of another tax advantage. There's a tax exemption for the profit you make from selling a house you have lived in for two of the previous five years. This means that if you live in any house for two of five years, you can sell it and not pay any federal tax on the gain. The limit is $250,000 per person, so couples get $500,000 in tax-free gain. Imagine fixing up a house and making over $100,000 or even more in profit, and then not paying any federal taxes on that profit. It is truly an amazing loophole for ordinary people.

Fix-and-flippers live in a house for two years while they fix it up. They hope to get an increase in value from improvements, along with an increase from appreciation or inflation. And finally, when they sell it they'll get up to $500,000 in tax-free profit.

What if the house hasn't gone up in value much after two years? Well, some flippers will buy a house, live in it for two years while they rehab it, and then immediately sell at the end of two years and take the gain tax-free and move to the next property. Others will live in the house for another two or three years and wait for its value to increase. That's because they can get the tax-free gain as long as they lived in the house two out of the previous five years.

Some flippers will live in the house for two years, and then move out and rent it to a tenant for three years. While they rent it, they can take advantage of the depreciation I discussed earlier. They get a tax write-off for another couple of years, while the renters cover all of the expenses. Then, after renting the house out for two to three years, they sell it. At that point, they will still get the tax-free gain because they lived in it for two of five years[47]. At the end of the day, they have a chunk of tax-free money, and then they do it again!

Some people will do this in twos. They will buy a house, fix it up for two years and then move out and rent out the first house. Then they buy a second house, live in it for two years and fix it up, and move on to a third house. At the end of the fourth or fifth year after they bought the first house, they'll sell it. This means they lived in it for two years (out of five) and then rented it for three more years, making rental income, depreciating it, and letting its value go up, and then when they sell it they don't pay federal tax on the gains. Then they have a second house being rented that they've already fixed up and lived in for two years, while they move on and do it again. Are you following all this? They can simply keep moving every two years, and selling one of their houses every two to three years, keeping the gains tax-free each time.

---

47 Note that you should consult your CPA about the timing and requirements for the "3 out of 5 year" rule. https://www.irs.gov/businesses/small-businesses-self-employed/sale-of-residence-real-estate-tax-tips

It's not for the lazy or risk-averse! If you do this, you'll have to move every few years. And of course it also means that you'll be living in a construction zone. You'll spend your evenings and weekends hanging drywall, painting, and swinging a hammer. But as a wealth building tool, there are few loopholes that are as effective for those who want to dig their way out of the moderate poverty and attain financial freedom.

Stepped-Up Basis

I've mentioned two tax reasons to use real estate to build wealth. One is depreciation. Another is the federal tax exemption from profit on your house as long as you've lived in it for two of the previous five years. But there's a third tax reason to invest in real estate: estate planning.

When you die, the heirs of your estate take the properties at their value at death, not what you paid for the properties. This isn't an estate tax loophole. It is a loophole for the gains you made by owning the property during your life.

For example, assume you paid $200,000 for a rental property in the year 2000. In 2020, you die and leave the property to your daughter. When you die in 2020, the property is worth $1 million. You technically made $800,000 in appreciation on the property. However, you didn't sell it. You left it to your daughter. She now has a rental property worth $1 million. She pays no gains tax on the increase from $200,000 to $1 million. If and when she sells it later, she will only pay gains on any increase in value over $1 million. That $800,000 is tax-free to you and to your heir. The basis in the property is "stepped up" from $200,000 to $1 million under a tax rule that makes the profit tax-free. If you had sold the property before you died, you would have paid taxes on the $800,000 in gains. If you just hold the property through death, then your heirs get a big payoff by skipping the tax gains you made while you were alive. Thus, owning real estate during life is a great way to build wealth. It's also a good way to pass on your wealth to your heirs.

Whether you own just enough rental property, or become a fix-and-flipper, I hope that you can see just how significant real estate is for people who want to get out of the rat race and rise from moderate poverty. I also hope you can see that getting into real estate can be done the scavenger way. You can bootleg and bootstrap your way into real estate the same as you can with getting into business.

The Risks

I've talked a lot about how amazing real estate can be as a tool for building wealth. Unfortunately, there are also risks with real estate, as with any investment. One big risk is that the market can be volatile, and even experience crashes. In 2007-2008 the real estate market took a massive hit that caused many people to let their homes go into foreclosure, file bankruptcy and lose everything. I personally lost a substantial sum in that crash. I survived the downturn by holding cash, borrowing, and even negotiating with my lenders to decrease interest. I held my properties through the crash until the value returned and sold at a gain. Many people were not so fortunate.

Market crashes can take many years to recover. As of the date of this writing, it has been ten years since the crash, and many markets are just now coming back. If you don't have the capacity to wait for such a recovery, then you should not undertake this type of investment.

You should avoid putting all your eggs into real estate. It is one pillar of the Opt Out life, and it should not be done without considering all risks. There are many great books on the subject, in addition to those already listed previously. Also, you should consult your financial advisors to ensure that the investments you make are proportionate to the risks you desire to accept.

In addition to the risks inherent in real estate, you should not substitute my ideas in this book for estate planning. Many people go through life with no will, no trust, and no plan for what might happen if they are in an accident that disables them or takes their lives. Adequate insurance and planning for these contingencies is essential, and are not part of this book.

There are also issues that each person must consider regarding assets that may be seized by creditors, or liquidated by Medicaid as part of the offset for costs incurred for long term care that exceeds the limit.

Please consider this book as one tool among many, and do not use it as a substitute for legal, accounting, and financial planning advice.

In addition to these risks, remember that it is quite possible to make bad real estate investments! You cannot assume that any property is a good investment. There are many books on real estate investing and you should become as conversant as you can on the subject before making an investment. Bad real estate can be a money pit that wipes you out. Good real estate investments can set you up for life. This pathway is one to be tread lightly.

Chapter Nine:
Making Your House an Asset

Last year, I received an email from an old friend who lives in Denmark. He had purchased a villa in the South of France, and invited my wife and I for a visit. "Come for a couple of weeks!" he wrote. Most Americans aren't free to take a couple of weeks to go hang out in France. With the Opt Out life, you can. And so I did.

If you ever get invited to go stay at someone's villa in the South of France, my advice is to take them up on it.

We landed at the airport in Nice on a warm July night and managed to get a rental car before dark. We mapped our route on Google Maps, and headed out. After an hour of winding roads, we finally came into a little village in the mountains above Saint Tropez. A village called La Garde Freinet was our destination.

I pulled the rental car to the side of the road to check the map, and a wild-looking man pulled up next to me and waved. He was in a topless 1975 Citroen automobile that looked like a beat-up

Volkswagen Thing. The man turned out to be my buddy Karl, his curly blonde hair blowing in the evening breeze. I rolled down my window and he shouted for me to follow him. A few minutes later we were behind the funky old convertible bouncing down a dirt road, through a gate into a gravel driveway and were soon sipping a cocktail on the veranda while kids played in the pool in the warm summer night air.

Karl's villa easily hosts a dozen guests, and we had a private room for the week. The massive house had a living room out of the pages of Architectural Digest®. The centerpiece was a turntable that connected to tube-amplified speakers. Karl's vinyl collection spans the decades, and includes Afrobeat, jazz, punk and EDM. The acoustics push the music throughout the villa and onto the outdoor patio, where a giant farm table stood with fourteen seats.

At the villa, our mornings included tennis on his private tennis court, and a dip in the pool before breakfast on the terrace overlooking miles of cork-oak forest. The area was once known for harvesting cork for wine bottles and, of course, wine.

In the cool of the evenings, we listened to old-school records. Karl played an old African djembe drum to the sound of an Afrobeat record that he found in a thrift store. He was a musician before he started his business, and he still enjoyed playing keyboard, guitar and percussion. The djembe drum resonated beautifully in the massive living room, where thick wooden beams crossed the high ceiling.

While most of the world is running in circles, trying to win the rat race, Karl is playing bocce ball with friends, sipping rose and playing cards at his farm table, or reading a book while his kids play in the pool.

This is the good life. Karl knows how to live. I've also been to his home in Denmark, where he lives in a posh flat in an expensive neighborhood. He has a vintage Peugeot in the garage. He travels extensively. He takes three weeks off each summer, and time off during the holidays, followed by a month of winter travel. In the past year, he's been to Italy, France, Asia and the U.S. for what appears to be nothing more than fun. He seems to have no wants. He has the quintessential lifestyle of the rich and famous.

I made the mistake of assuming that Karl was simply rich. I assumed he was like so many other wealthy Europeans who have boats moored at San Tropez or Cannes, like the other rich people who have villas in the south of France. The reality is that Karl created this life by opting out. He didn't inherit any money. He didn't sell a company for millions. He's made a conscious choice to opt out, and to not play by the rules.

Karl owns a business, a side gig and real estate. That's how he generates income. When it comes to his expenses, he's not just writing checks for a lavish lifestyle. He uses alternative currencies to buy goods and services. While he is on vacation in France, he rents his Danish apartment to an American family through AirBnB. The Americans are paying Karl $5,000 for three weeks at Karl's Denmark flat. He's making money on his primary residence while he's taking a vacation in the South of France. And, that villa in the south of France generates sizable rent from vacationers when Karl isn't using it. He only uses it personally about six weeks out of the year. The rest of the time, it's generating income to pay the mortgage. These Opt Out principles work whether you are in the U.S. or Europe or Asia. The Opt Out life works whether you want to vagabond the world, or want to sip rose on the terrace of your Mediterranean villa.

Karl's buddy Marcus is jealous of Karl's life. You might be as well. But to be jealous is to misunderstand Karl's success. His life does not come from good luck. Karl isn't "fortunate" as we often think of rich people being. He's doing the same subversive things that I'm writing about in this book.

Karl's good friend Marcus doesn't get it. Marcus thinks Karl is just rich. Marcus is jealous, and he wants to live Karl's life. But Marcus also has a large fancy house, and likes to take expensive vacations. Marcus buys nice things he thinks are symbolic of success, like his $10,000 Rolex®. When Marcus goes on vacation, he doesn't want to rent out his home to some tourist. So he generates no income from it to offset his vacation costs. Marcus is too nervous to start a business, so he's stuck in a job that he hates. His wife works at a regular job as well. They feel that it is beneath them to have a "side gig." Marcus will never have the life that Karl has, even though he and his wife both have good jobs and live in a nice home. They haven't opted out. Karl has.

Thus far we've talked about income pillars. Owning a business, having a side gig, and owning rental property are the three income pillars.

When it comes to expenses, I have three pillars as well:

1. Make your home an asset

2. Use cashless currencies

3. Scavenge

This chapter and the next focus on how to make your home an asset. That's one of the three ways you'll change how your expenses impact your life.

Whether you've traveled to the mountains for a visit to the snow, or stayed at the beach for a week in the summer, you've probably rented a house or condo on AirBnB or Homeaway's VRBO system. You may have even taken a trip abroad and stayed in a vacation rental: paying to use someone's house or condo for a few days or even a few weeks.

If you haven't used a vacation rental, then you are probably missing out on a great way to travel. Renting a house or apartment gives you a deeper travel experience than staying in a fancy hotel, and often it is far cheaper. You get to feel like a local, and often stay in a regular neighborhood, rather than a stale hotel.

Even if you have used a vacation rental as a tenant, you may not have considered renting your own house out through AirBnB or VRBO. Renting a room in your house short-term can create an amazing income, and enables you to meet new people from all over the world.

As you know by now, your house is not an asset, it's a liability. We want to find ways to make it an asset. I've already covered the first way: You can be a live-in-fix-up-flipper and reside in your home for two years while you fix it up, and then sell it and keep the capital gains tax-free. The other way is to rent it out when you aren't there, or rent part of it even while you are there.

Rent a Sofa, a Room, or More

If you are not occupying all the rooms in your house, you have the potential to make some income from that space. For starters, you can consider renting a room full-time. A graduate student might pay to rent a room in your house, and never bother you. In San Diego, a room can fetch $800 per month or more. That's an easy way to generate significant cash, while still living in your home.

But many people, including me, don't want to have a full-time tenant in our home. Vacation rental platforms such as AirBnB allow you to generate income without taking on a full-time roommate.

I was out one night with my buddy Carlos. He's a 30-year-old entrepreneur who owns a condo in downtown San Diego. He and I hit a concert one evening near downtown.

"I can drop you at your condo," I said.

"Actually, no thanks. I can't use my apartment tonight." he replied.

"What?" I exclaimed. "Do you have a plumbing problem or something?"

"Oh. No. No," he said. "I've rented it for three nights on AirBnB. I'm getting $500, which covers half of my mortgage."

"Wait," I said. "You are paying half your mortgage with three nights of rental income?"

"Oh, yeah. In fact, I typically rent it enough each month to pay the whole mortgage," he said. "But that means I've got to crash at a friend's house when my place is rented."

"No way," I replied. "You are paying your whole mortgage and you just have to vagabond for six nights each month?"

"Yup," Carlos said shyly. "It's one reason I keep the place. It pays for itself, and I still get to use it most of the month."

I was amazed. This young man could turn his condo into a money-maker and all he had to do was go use a friend's sofa or spare room every now and then. He told me that he usually spent the night at a friend's house when he would go out on weekends anyhow. So the fact that he did this five or six nights each month did not create a burden. He also had the flexibility to determine when he was willing to rent his condo. He could look at each rental inquiry and determine if it was convenient for him to move out for a few days.

I'm sure there were times when it was an inconvenience for Carlos. But he was making $1,000 per month, and using that money to cover his entire mortgage. If he does this for a few years, he may reach a point where he has saved enough money to buy another condo, and he can rent his first one more often and generate even more money.

You can also short-term rent a room in your house. You may not have to move out like Carlos did. Instead, rent your sofa on a short time basis to a couch surfer. AirBnB allows you to list your couch, room or entire house to short-term travelers. Consider the difference between renting a room to a college student for $800 for a month versus renting the same room for $50 to $100 per night. The benefit is that you can make the same $800 in eight days rather than hosting a tenant in your space full-time. In addition to AirBnB, you can use VRBO.com, or its network of vacation rental sites, to offer your home for rent to vacationers.

You can also do what Karl does: rent your house or condo while you take a vacation for a few weeks. I did this once and it paid for my entire month in Europe.

Maybe you're worried about someone trashing your house or hosting an orgy. I've been doing short-term rentals for over 20 years and have never seen a house get trashed or suffer major damage. Truth be told, there was one group that left a footprint on the bedroom wall ... about four feet up. It's still a mystery, but the cost to touch up the paint was minimal. It is much more likely that you will meet cool people and make some cold, hard cash than to have someone cause damage to your home.

Short-term renting increases your income and thus, makes your home an asset rather than just a liability. What else can you do to make your house an asset? Let's look at a couple more ideas.

Build a Fonzie Flat

Remember Happy Days? Ugh, I'm dating myself here! Well, way back when television was actually on a television set, and when you needed an antenna to actually see anything on television, there was a show called Happy Days. It was a sitcom about family life in the 1950s. The Cunninghams had a suburban home with a studio apartment in the attic. The studio apartment had its own entrance. Henry Winkler's character Arthur Fonzerelli (aka "Fonzie") rented the flat.

One great way to make your home into an income-producing asset is to create a Fonzie Flat. You can use a spare room with an external door, or an attic space. Even if your Fonzie Flat doesn't have a kitchen, a student or young professional might rent your Fonzie Flat without a kitchen. When he was a student, one of my long-time friends once rented a studio with no kitchen. He used a two-burner electric stovetop to cook, and a small extra sink to wash his dishes. He thought it was perfect, and the homeowners loved having the extra income. You as the homeowner can rent a Fonzie Flat to grad students who are respectful and just need something economical for a season of life. You don't have to turn your studio into the Four Seasons! There's a large market for something that's less than luxurious, and it doesn't mean you'll be renting to unemployed hippies.

How much can you make from your Fonzie Flat? In San Diego, it can fetch $1,000 per month if you rent long-term, or $3,000 to 4,000 per month if you rent it on a short term basis. Stop for a minute and digest this. You can do well if you just create a Fonzie Flat and rent it to a college student or a young professional for $1,000 a month. That sort of income can change your life. It may enable you to pay off your mortgage in 10 years rather than 30 years. But consider the massive increase in income you could create if you rent your Fonzie Flat out to short-term vacationers. What would it mean for you to make $30,000 or even more each year from having a little studio that you rent behind your house? I've done this. And it works. Whether you rent long-term or short-term, the Fonzie Flat is the ideal way to monetize your home and make it an asset.

A long-term renter will generally sign a six- or 12-month lease. That provides a steady flow of extra cash from your home. There's generally not much work involved in a long-term rental. Most people who rent their Fonzie Flat long-term find that it's hands-off, and well worth the income.

If you want to rent your Fonzie Flat on a short-term basis, then there's a bit more work involved. You need to furnish the flat. You need to market the flat. And you need to manage and process the income. You'll also need to have a cleaning person come in after each rental and get it clean and ready for the next guest. For some, this will be too much work. If it's too daunting for you, then just long-term rent the unit to a grad student. If you don't mind the additional work of furnishing, marketing and cleaning, then research on whether you can rent your Fonzie Flat to people coming to your town on vacation. You can do this by checking for other similar properties on VRBO.com or AirBnB.com. If others near you are successfully renting their spare rooms, studios, and homes, then you can too. Just create your own account on any of these websites, and start renting your Fonzie Flat nightly. For example, one of my Fonzie Flats rented for $125 per night. It rented about 20 nights per month. That's $2,500 per month for a small unit behind my house. I would only have made $1,000 if it was a long-term rental. The extra $1,500 a month was well worth the extra work.

There's an additional benefit to a short-term rental unit: It provides down time when you have no tenants. That means no one parking in front of your house, no one passing back and forth on your side yard, and no one walking around up in your attic space. If you rent a Fonzie Flat for 60 percent of the month, you'll make more money than having a permanent tenant, and then you'll have 40 percent of the time without anyone in your extra space. You can allow your friends and family to use the space when it is not being rented out. The Fonzie Flat can become your guesthouse, and make having guests far more fun. Your mother-in-law might appreciate the extra space when she visits, and you might appreciate the buffer, too.

Short-term renters can become more than just visitors; they can become fast friends. I've met guests from around the world, and had return visitors who come back year after year. You may find yourself having a glass of wine with an interesting traveler from an exotic city. AirBnB has a good track record of keeping problematic people from renting in its network. In addition, the rental platforms (AirBnB and HomeAway, for example) have the personal information of your guest, which provides an element of security.

There's another significant benefit of the Fonzie Flat. You use it for trades. It becomes a powerful form of non-cash currency. You can trade a week in your Fonzie Flat to someone who owns a condo in the mountains, or an apartment in Munich. How would you like to take a free vacation in the mountains every winter? Or use someone's flat in Paris? I talk about how to trade the use of your whole house as a way to travel in Chapter 11. And having a Fonzie Flat means you don't need to swap your whole house. You can just swap your Fonzie Flat for the use of someone else's flat. Even more important is that you can swap the use of your flat for someone's cabin or condo and not have to make the trade during the exact same time the way you would if you were doing a house-for-house swap. You can let someone stay in your flat in June, and you can use a week in their cabin in January. If you have a Fonzie Flat that you rent short-term, you have total flexibility.

In the next chapter, I'll tell you how I once paid for most of my rent from the income on my Fonzie Flat. Imagine paying all of your mortgage from short-term rental income, but without moving out of your house, and without having renters inside your home. Even cutting your rent or mortgage in half can be well worth it. When you take the savings you get from the rental of your Fonzie Flat, and combine it with your side gig income, your entire life will begin to change. If you want to launch a business, having a side gig and Fonzie Flat income will give you the extra cash to do that, without borrowing or seeking investors. The income and expense pillars that allow you to opt out are interwoven. The more pillars you implement, the greater the impact on your life.

Rent Your Entire House Short-Term

Consider renting your house out while you vacation, like my buddy Karl. If you have a reason to be out of your house for a week or longer, you can rent it while you are gone. I talk more about this in Chapter 11, as a way of enabling travel. Even if you don't use this as a travel hack, you can make extra income on your house by renting it when you are out of town on business, or visiting family and your home is vacant. Remember my buddy Carlos? He would accept rentals of his condo on an ad hoc basis, and then use a friend's spare room or sofa for those nights. You don't have to be quite as flexible! You might have plans to see your grandmother, or a business trip in another state, or a vacation. You can rent your house or condo while you take those trips, and make quite a bit of extra money while you are away.

My friend Kevin decided to vacation-rent his spare bedroom. He spent a few years as a bachelor and found that it was a fun way to make extra money. Plus, he loved having house-guests. His friendly dog loved it as well. In the years that Kevin rented his spare room to vacationers, he never had a problem, and even had repeat guests. If you live near a college or university, you'll find that the renters are often parents who come to spend time with their kids, and don't want to stay in a hotel.

You might feel that this is dangerous, or that people will steal your things. This may happen in rare instances. However, most vacation rental transactions go smoothly and without damage. In addition, you can do a few things to help manage the risks. First, you can put your valuable things into one or two closets and install locks. One summer I rented my house for two weeks for $10,000 and used that money to travel in Europe with my family. I put locks on four closet doors, and then a lock on the basement. I moved the valuables to the locked spaces, and then let the nice family from Arizona come use my house for their vacation. For $10,000 it was well worth the risk, and at the end of the month, there was no damage, no theft, and they asked if they could rent our house again the following year.

You can insure against damage by requiring a damage waiver policy that can be provided by vacation rental insurance companies. Also, some vacation rental websites offer the ability to add damage waiver insurance when the party reserves your house. For one condo I own, I charge $50.00 for a damage waiver that covers insurance up to $1,500 in damage. I've only had to use it twice in ten years, both times for accidental broken chairs. I could live without it, but it is a nice additional assurance.

Finally, you can be cautious about who you rent to. Find out a little more about the prospective tenant and what the purpose of his or her vacation is. Only rent to adults over a certain age to help avoid your house becoming the MTV Beach House for a frat party. Again, there are some risks, but the reward is generally far greater.

House Swap for Vacation

Another item I cover in Chapter 12 is swapping your house for someone else's house for vacation. There are many websites that allow you to list your house for trade, along with the dates you would like to travel. You might want to be gone all of August and visit the Spanish coast, and a nice Spanish family may want to spend August in the U.S. and trade houses with you for the same period.[48] In one sense, swapping doesn't put money directly in your pocket like a vacation rental on AirBnB. However, you will be saving money that you would otherwise spend if you paid for a hotel. Swapping for vacation is part of making your home an asset, rather than a liability, while not diminishing your lifestyle. In fact, you should be able to see by now that my plan for you to opt out of the rat race isn't about dropping out and living off the grid, or by urban scavenging. Your lifestyle should improve with my approach. Your new life should have more freedom, more travel, and more income, all while diminishing your stress, and eventually breaking you free of moderate American poverty.

---

48 Think you can't take a month off to travel in Europe? That's part of the Opt Out life. Follow the income and expense pillars and you'll be doing that and more.

Rent Your Unused Space

In some cities, a garage is golden. A single parking place in Boston recently went on the market for $650,000.[49] People pay substantial sums to rent parking spots, garage space and storage units. You can consider renting all or part of your garage for someone to store tools, a car, a trailer. You might even be able to charge a small fee to allow someone you know to rent a partial space above your garage for storing things they don't have room for. You will be monetizing empty space and helping a friend. Attic space. Do you have a shed in the back yard? Think creatively about the space you have and whether someone might pay you, even a small sum, to use some of that space for storage.

I own a four-plex that had a spare garage. The garage was extra-long, and that made it undesirable to rent for the full value of the size. So I divided the garage into two spaces with a wall. Half is a garage and half is now my own storage space (saving over $175 a month). I then found a guy who needed to rent a garage, and rented him the garage portion for $175 a month. I'm making $175 in rental income and I'm saving $175 that I was previously paying for mini storage. The value of that $350 per month can grow to $100,000 in less than 15 years.[50]

---

49 http://fusion.net/story/226768/boston-parking-space-most-expensive/
50 If you take that $350 per month for 15 years and put it into an investment making a 6% return, it results in over $100,000.

Make it Produce Something Beautiful

In Chapter 4, I talked about Cory's side gig being a small recording studio in his garage. He has turned his house into an asset. Not only does the side gig pay him more than his mortgage, it is enough to generate excess income as well. He had to invest in the build-out of his studio, but it has paid for itself many times over. Your garage can become a sound studio, or a studio for artwork, or even woodwork. Will others pay to share your wood shop tools? Can you rent your garage to a small band to practice each week? You make extra money, and get free live entertainment!

Get Solar

These days you can use your house to generate your own electricity with solar panels. This not only can reduce your electrical bill to zero, but you can sell electricity back to the utility. Many states offer tax rebates and tax credits, and federal programs have come and gone and continue to be offered in one iteration or another. Look carefully into the programs and do the math to see if it is worth your investment to make your house an independent power source, and even make money back from the power company.

You can go solar with water heating systems to save money on hot water. What about your water bill? I've known people who employ their own gray water system that uses their sink water for yard and garden irrigation. They save hundreds of dollars every year by re-routing their sink water to repurpose as irrigation for the yard.

Anything you can do that significantly reduces your monthly obligations will make your house a better investment and not just another source of expense.

Renting vs. Buying

I haven't spent much time talking about home ownership directly at this point. I've talked about how a home is not an asset, but that once you pay off your home, it is an important part of your retirement strategy. I've also talked about how to make your home an asset. But I haven't focused on homeownership because part of taking the Opt Out path is to diminish the importance of owning your home. In order to eventually own your dream home, you have to choose a different path than the one society tells you about. You can't rush off and buy a home and think that this is how you will get ahead financially. Instead, step back and consider the strategies in this book. You can, and will, achieve home ownership as a piece to the overall strategy, but it is not the only one, and it is not necessarily the most important one.

That's right, you don't need to own your home. In fact, it is often the best strategy to own a home that you rent out to others, and to pay to rent the home that you live in. Again, the home you live in is a liability, it is costing you money to own! Your home does not generate income, and therefore it is not technically an asset. Don't make home ownership the top priority. If you do own a home, then look for ways to make it an asset.

There have been times in my life when I owned the home I lived in, and many times when I didn't own my home, but leased it from someone else. The reason is that owning a home is not always the best use of my money. For example, I owned and lived in a condo for a year before I realized that I could rent it out and make a lot of extra cash, and then use that cash to rent a nice house in a better neighborhood for my family. That move meant that I could still own the condo, but by renting it out I was able to use the excess cash flow to pay the rent on a house. I lived rent-free as a result because the rent was paid by the excess income from renting my condo. And the house I rented had ocean views and was worth over $1 million. It would have been a terrible financial decision to buy the $1 million house, and start paying a giant mortgage and property taxes of $7,000 a month, when I could simply rent the same house for just $2,500 and pay for it with the excess income from my other property.

Do you see how this approach is contrary to what you have been taught about home ownership? You've been told that you should work hard, save some money and then buy the biggest house you can afford. You then end up strapped into a 30-year mortgage that you can barely afford, to buy a house that doesn't make you any money. This is a trap that I want you to avoid.

Of course, owning a home is fine, and should be part of your overall goal of financial independence. Let me talk about strategies for home ownership.

When you do want to buy a house, consider buying a home that already has a Fonzie Flat. I've explained why earlier in this chapter. You can also consider buying a multi-unit property and living in one of the units. For example, you could purchase a three- or four-unit apartment complex using conventional lending programs that are as easy to get as a typical home loan. Consider a house that has two additional units over the garage or on the same property. You can live in the house and rent the two units, generating cash flow that covers part or all of your cost of ownership. Over time, as rent increases, you'll be able to move out and rent the unit you've been using as your home, and buy another home. The rent from all three of the units will then be used to cover the mortgage on your next house. Can you see how this works out better for you in the long run than just buying a large single-family house? You don't need to work a job you hate if your mortgage is covered by your rental property. You get to opt out of the system, and still have everything you dreamed about.

What about buying when the market is down? The timing of your purchase is an issue to consider, but not as important as you may think. You cannot expect to buy at the bottom and sell at the top. I've only done this once, and it was not because I was a genius. It was luck. You will want to buy at a time when you are ready, and not in a contrived effort try to time the market. Buy when you can qualify for a loan, and when you are not likely to require a major move in your near future.

You certainly should avoid buying into a frenzied market, with buyers making crazy offers and people driven by speculation.

What is more important than timing is to be sure that you are realistic about the value. The best way to determine if you are getting a realistic value is to look at the rental market for the house you are buying. Consider whether you could pay your mortgage, taxes and insurance if you were to buy the house and then immediately rent it out. If so, then you are probably buying in a value range that makes sense, even if you don't rent it out. You know that you could rent it out if necessary, and thus, it confirms that the house is a reasonable investment.

What if you don't want a house with a Fonzie Flat, and you don't want to live in a triplex? Buy a house that you can easily afford, and one that will become a good rental property when you eventually move out. Don't buy the biggest thing you can afford. Buy something that will make a great rental property in ten or twenty years. That way, when you do eventually move into something else, you can keep the smaller property and easily let the rental income pay the expenses and even put money in your pocket.

I hope you see that the Opt Out approach of real estate and home ownership gets you more of the American Dream than if you stay in the rat race and play by the rules. I'm advocating a lifestyle of resourcefulness that ultimately gets you a lot more: a bigger house and more money, while also providing you with a pathway to gain financial freedom. You don't have to work at a corporate job for thirty years just to pay off that big suburban McMansion. You can use these tools to end up with a house that pays for itself, and eventually pays you perpetually.

Don't forget that you can write off your home office if you use it exclusively for operating your business. That means you may be able to expense a portion of your mortgage (or rent), utilities, and insurance based on using a dedicated space for your office. If you have a Fonzie Flat or other business use of your home, you can also use a different room as your home office, and get the additional tax benefit associated with your home office deductions.

Chapter Ten:
Living Rent-Free

In the last chapter, I told you about how to make your home an income-generating asset. I hinted at how I've used the same principles to live rent-free. For many people, the only way they can imagine living rent-free is to move back in with their parents! Remember, I'm not telling you how to live a smaller life, or live on a budget. I'm proposing a life that is bigger than you can imagine, not a life where you live in your parents' basement.

For me to live rent-free, I've had to rethink what it means to be a homeowner. I've had to opt out of the social stigma of renting. You don't need to own a home! Not yet. You can wait until you've risen from moderate poverty and buy a house or condo later. As you've already read, I've owned property and I still do. I just don't own the house I live in. That's a key concept. You want to own real estate that generates rental income.

What I am saying here may seem like sacrilege to most people. Everyone thinks that the first thing a young professional should do is buy a home. But as we've discussed, a home is not an asset unless you find a way to make it generate income. Your home is a liability. It costs you something to live in it.

Even though I can afford to own a home, I have chosen to advance my financial position through renting, rather than owning the house I live in. And even the rent that I do pay is offset by other income from a Fonzie Flat or other property. I'll walk you through my unique housing choices, and show you how I lived in a multimillion-dollar house with sweeping ocean views for six years, how I lived in a million-dollar house that was four lots up from the ocean for five years; and how I lived in an oceanfront condo for three years rent-free. I used different strategies for each. But the net effect was that I spent 15 of the past 20 years living in beautiful places worth over $1 million each, while not paying anything. You can, too!

Beach Condo

Let me start with the oceanfront condo.

I approached the owners of a small beachfront complex in 1996 and asked if they needed an on-site manager. It was a complete shot in the dark. I had no knowledge of whether the owners used a manager, or if they needed one. I just knew that I wanted to live rent-free and this seemed like a possible opportunity. Why not ask? I called Tom, the owner, and said, "Do you happen to need a manager?" He replied, "Actually, yes, we do need a manager."

I was shocked. He invited me to come down for a few upcoming weekends to get to know the property.

Note that this opportunity did not fall into my lap. I had to think creatively and be bold enough to make that phone call. If you want to find opportunity, you'll have to hustle. You'll need to ask and be turned down. You'll feel embarrassed. Don't let these things keep you from finding the opportunities that may change your life. Don't be passive and just wait for a door to open. Go out and push on those doors and make something happen. Have the audacity to reach out.

Before I landed the manager job, I had to prove myself to Tom. I spent several weeks helping clean up the property on the weekends for free. This allowed Tom and his sister to get to know me. After I proved that I was the right kind of person for the job, they hired me. I negotiated a deal to let me live in one of the two-bedroom apartments. As pay for my role as property manager, I only paid half of the going rental rate. Not bad, right? I also negotiated a bonus. If I kept the property fully occupied I would have the remainder of the rent wiped out as well. I did keep the property occupied, and thus paid no rent, living on the beach for three years for free.

This apartment complex rented to college students during the school year, and then vacation renters during the summer. The owners needed a manager who could play tough guy to the students, and nice guy to the vacationers. My wife and I made a good team for this. I was the bad cop and she was the good cop. It also

helped that I could fix and repair a few things to keep the maintenance costs down.

The best feature of this deal was not the free rent, it was the fact
that the whole apartment complex was directly on the beach in
San Diego, California. For three years we raised our daughter
with the ocean as her playground. She learned to ride a bike on
the boardwalk. We took walks on the beach each morning with
our coffee, hunting for seashells. Rather than paying rent, we
simply performed our duties as managers. We even made a little
extra money from doing additional work around the property.

I can't guarantee that you are going to land a gig like this, on the
beach. I can say that many property owners would be happy to
have a young energetic entrepreneur helping manage their apartments. For hustlers who want to climb their way out of moderate
poverty, property management is a great thing to do, at least for
a season while you are saving and getting ready to launch a business. You can use this type of job to get a season of free rent, while
the property owner gets a solid manager who is honest and hard-
working.

I've owned several apartment complexes of my own. I struggled
to find good on-site managers for my apartments. In fact, managers are so hard to find that I often put up with substandard
managers for years. I've had terrible managers. This means there
is a great opportunity for you hard-working entrepreneurs to get
free rent for a season of your life.

Managing apartments isn't the only way to get free rent. There are also other ways to be resourceful when it comes to housing. Let me give you some other ideas based on what I've done.

Beach Cottage

In Chapter 11, I will cover a financial strategy that I call "shifting." The idea of shifting is to take something that you are spending one way, and then redirect it for your greater financial advancement. For example, if you own rental property, you get to write-off depreciation. That shifts money you would pay to the IRS to yourself through a tax loophole. Another shifting method is where you purchase or lease a car through your business, which also saves money on taxes. You can also shift when it comes to housing. I'll use one of my experiences as an example. But I must share some backstory so that you understand how I ended up not paying anything to live in a quaint three-bedroom house that was four lots back from the ocean.

In Chapter 8, I told you about how I purchased a $330,000 condo on the beach by hustling to get the money for the down payment. Well, I moved into that condo for a year. It was a great place to live because I could walk on the beach, ride my bike to restaurants and bars, and live the coastal life. But it was located in a dense vacation rental zone. Because of its proximity to the beach, it was congested with tourists part of the year and with students another part of the year. One night I was awakened at 2 a.m. by the sound of an electric guitar playing Stairway to Heaven. The sound was not me dreaming that I was at a Led Zeppelin concert, but a drunk student living in the next building, who felt it was time to play his electric guitar on the patio. I was scheduled to be up for an early flight in just a few hours. My night's sleep was ruined. I decided I was too old for this shit, and that it was time to find a neighborhood with more working adults. Before I could move to a quieter neighborhood, I had to figure out how to pay for it.

Follow along. I'm going to explain how I kept the condo, and used the financial principle that I call shifting to get myself into a great house where I didn't have to listen to electric guitar riffs at 2 a.m.

My condo payment (and property tax) was about $1,600 per month. I wanted to live in a single-family house in La Jolla, a rather expensive suburb, and where my daughter was already enrolled in school. If I bought a small house in La Jolla it would have cost over $1 million. To buy a $1 million house, I'd have to put down $200,000 and then carry payments of about $7,000 per month. I couldn't afford that. Renting would be the only way to go for now.

So I started house hunting. Rents were $4,000 to $7,000 per month. Yikes! I kept an eye on the market, hoping to find a deal. One day my wife looked at a house we were passing in the car, and said, "That one looks nice, and also looks vacant." I shrugged it off as likely too expensive. It was perched on a slope, just a few houses up from the ocean, and above one of the best surf spots in San Diego. You could see the waves crashing, and smell the salt air. You could see whale spouts off on the horizon where the sun glimmered on the expansive Pacific Ocean.

That evening, I was scouring the online listings and also the MLS (which I can access as a licensed real estate broker). Among the very expensive homes listed for $4,000 per month and up, I found exactly one listing for $2,500. It was the very house my wife had pointed at earlier that day! I love serendipity. I made an appointment to view the house, and locked it down.

But I had a problem. I could only afford what I was already paying in mortgage, which was about $1,600. I was not ready to pay $2,500 per month! That would be an increase of nearly $1,000 per month in my cost of living. I knew I could afford $1,600, but not more.

Here's what I did. My condo was in an ideal location to rent to vacationers. Remember, it was a condo down by the ocean where vacationers pay high prices for short-term stays. My condo was nicely furnished. So I did a little math. It turned out that the condo could generate about $3,000 per month on average as a vacation rental. My mortgage (with other expenses) was a bit under $2,000 per month. I figured out that I could rent the condo as a short-term rental, and have a net gain of $1,000 per month. I could use that $1,000 per month to offset my new rent of $2,500 and only end up with an effective monthly rent of $1,500. Living in my condo cost me about $1,600 per month, and living in the rented house would cost a net sum of $1,500 per month. My monthly rent would go down by $100 per month, and I could live in a mature neighborhood with no students playing electric guitar in the middle of the night! Even better, the house was walking distance to my daughter's school. The house had sweeping ocean views. Yes, I still paid rent, but remember that I was able to shift what I was paying, make a $1,000 per month gain, and even reduce my monthly budget, all while living in a $1 million house.

What I did was employ a shift, a financial maneuver that allowed me to keep the condo as an investment, keep the mortgage payment covered, and use the excess cash to offset the cost of renting a better house. My lifestyle improved, and my cost of living went down.

But that's not the end. After living in that wonderful house for five years, I upped my lifestyle even more, and decreased my cost of living again! Let's talk about my next move.

The Street of Dreams

The town of La Jolla is known as "The Jewel" of San Diego. It is a beautiful hillside village hugging the Pacific Ocean, about 12 miles north of downtown San Diego. One of the nicest streets is Camino de la Costa; also known as the "Street of Dreams." Most of the homes are quite large and they range in price from $4 million to over $20 million. Nothing on this street is cheap. Every home is beautiful. We lived only a few blocks from this street, and walked our dog along the Street of Dreams every day. But I never expected to live on that street.

One day, my wife noticed that one of the homes on this street was having an estate sale. Someone elderly must have passed away, or had moved into care. We decided to investigate, and also scavenge around the estate sale for bargains. We asked the people who were hosting the estate sale about the house. It turned out that the elderly owner needed full-time care, and the family wanted to lease the house and use the funds to pay for her care. I hunted down the owner and ended up negotiating a long-term lease. The rent would be $5,250 per month.

Remember, my budget was $1,500 per month. I could afford more, but I really didn't want to have to pay more if I didn't have to. So what was I thinking, getting into a long-term lease at $5,250? I had a plan.

First, let me tell you about the house. It was a large Spanish style home built in 1927 at a time when the neighborhood had not yet been established, and it was one of the first houses built on the Street of Dreams. It was one lot back from the ocean with unobstructed views of the Pacific. There were five fireplaces, one of which was as tall as my wife and five feet wide. You could roast a pig in that fireplace. Did I mention I love sitting by the fire? I digress. Original wrought iron sconces adorned the walls, and one great room had a barrel ceiling 22 feet high, crossed with ornamental ironwork and giant wrought iron trusses. There was a den with another fireplace; I set up my office in it, and hung antique animal trophies on the walls. There was a formal dining room, equipped with an old, but functional system to ring the maid from the table with a foot button. One of the bedrooms also

199

had a buzzer to ring the kitchen, just in case you didn't want to walk all the way from the bedroom wing to the kitchen for a late-night sandwich. Of course I didn't have a maid, so I had to make my own sandwiches.

There was a beautiful interior courtyard with a built-in outdoor fireplace (yeah, another fireplace), and a charming fountain. Flowers climbed the walls and I strung little white lights across the courtyard to give it a warm glow in the evenings. Above the garage was a studio apartment, possibly once used for a driver, or a housekeeper.

The studio was the reason I knew I could afford this house. It would be my Fonzie Flat.

That little chauffeur studio was a rentable unit. I didn't have a chauffeur, so I knew I could make extra income by subletting it to offset my new giant monthly lease payment. How much could I rent it for? Well, it might have only rented for $1,000 or $1,200 per month as a long-term rental. But remember that part of opting out is looking for for unseen value. What is a studio apartment worth ... to me? Try $4,000 per month as a short-term rental. I've already told you how to rent a Fonzie Flat on AirBnB or VRBO. Remember that beach condo from the story above? It would have only rented for $2,000 per month as a long-term rental. But we made $3,000 per month from it because we offered it as a short-term vacation rental. This little studio apartment above the garage was charming, and had ocean views. It would make for a great vacation rental. At $150 per night, even renting it 20 nights out of 30, that little studio could generate upwards of

$3,000 per month. But we knew we could do even better. And we did.

With my lease payment at $5,250, and offset by income of $4,000, my effective rent was going to be $1,250 to rent a mansion on the Street of Dreams that otherwise was worth at least $2 million. Now, remember that the previous base rent I was paying was $1,500 ($2,500 minus the $1,000 excess from my beach condo). Now I was going to go from paying an effective cost of $1,500 per month, to paying $1,250 minus $1,000 in beach condo income. I was going to live in the mansion for $250 per month. In fact, by this point, the beach condo income had risen, meaning that I was living in the Spanish mansion for … wait for it … free.

I was living in a beautiful house on the most luxurious street and effectively not paying a dime. I did this for more than six years! Imagine living rent-free in a fancy neighborhood, and not being a millionaire. If I did it, you can, too. I even used the house to pay for an extended European vacation. I mentioned this story briefly already, but will reiterate it here.

One summer, I rented the main house to a farmer from Arizona for two weeks while I took a vacation. The farmer paid $10,000 for two weeks. This was actually a bargain compared to other summer rentals in the area. My month-long vacation in Europe with my family cost $5,000. I netted $5,000 after paying for a month of traveling in Europe and even had a wonderful farmer and his family essentially paying for the privilege to watch over the house while I was gone!

You may not want to rent your entire house to a stranger from Arizona for two weeks. But renting a separate room or studio can cover your entire lease or mortgage. Renting a studio or back bedroom of your home to vacationers sounds dangerous and crazy. What about having tenants in your space, or damage, or problems? In six years, I never had a problem; no injuries, no complaints, no damage. Rather than problems, I made some friends, and had guests from all over the world who were happy to stay in the little studio apartment. And I lived the life of a millionaire in a seaside mansion.

This seems too good to be true, right? Surely Dana and Heather got lucky with this once-in-a-lifetime opportunity … right? Absolutely not. After that property was sold and we moved, I did the very same thing again with a different property. The opportunities are out there! You can find these types of deals if you are willing to be creative. Opt out of what others tell you. Opt out of the need to own a home. Opt into a new life, one that you determine, one that takes you into the life you've been dreaming of.

Of course, be mindful of whether you can legally rent a part of a house you own or rent. In some cities, short-term rentals are regulated. In the case of renting, if you lease a property, it is wisest to ask in advance whether you can rent out a room or unit as part of your overall deal. Having done this multiple times, I can tell you that I've had it work out just fine, and I've also had it backfire. The opportunities abound, if only you decide to opt out of the traditional view about renting or owning a home, and look for unique opportunities like I did.

Finding a way to live in an amazing house or apartment cheap or even free is a matter of being creative and opening your mind to the possibilities. You must think outside the box. That's what it means to opt out of the American mentality. You can't sit back, or mope around and say, "I'm poor, I can't afford to live in an awesome house at the beach." Wherever you are and whatever background you come from, you must open your mind. The greatest limits are the ones we put on ourselves. Twenty years ago, I would never have envisioned that I could live in an ocean-front condo for free ... or that seaside cottage for $1,500 per month ... or the Spanish mansion for free. I had to open my mind to the possibility, and then look for opportunity.

I hope my stories illustrate what's possible for you. Once you see the possibilities, you can open up to situations that otherwise would feel out of your reach. They're not. But first you must make that subtle mental shift. It's everything. I hope I've helped you make that mental shift through my personal stories. I'm not saying, "This is what I did, and you should do it as well." I'm using my stories to help open your mind to what is possible for you. I truly believe that you can do far more amazing things than I've done if you open your mind to the possibilities.

Chapter Eleven:
Cashless Currencies

Thus far I've given you three income strategies: a side gig, a business, and real estate.

My three expense pillars are: make your home an asset, use cashless currencies, and scavenge. In the previous chapter, I covered my concepts for making your home an asset, and how you can live cheaply, or even free, when it comes to renting your home. Now we are moving into my second expense strategy: using cashless currencies.

To opt out, you have to start thinking about money differently. You want to hold onto your cash, and find other ways to pay for things, aside from traditional currency. I'm not talking about cryptocurrency here. I'm talking about ways to pay for lifestyle without using any monetary currency.

Money — digital or otherwise — is just one form of currency. Once you realize that you have other currencies, you can use those to enhance your life. Remember, the Opt Out life is not about living on a budget, or scaling back your lifestyle. I want you to live the good life. In this section, you'll learn to expand your ability to live well by using non-cash currencies, rather than always using your cash.

Non-cash currencies are some of the most important concepts for bootstrappers, scavengers and subversives who have opted out of the system. When you stop viewing cash as your only currency, you learn that you can acquire goods and services in many ways that don't use cash. The ideas here go beyond the simple concept of bartering that you might learn from, say, The Tightwad Gazette, or your freegan dumpster-diving buddy. Wealthy people use non-monetary currency for a variety of things that increase their lifestyle without deploying cash. Let's learn how to look for currency in other places than your wallet or bank account.

Trading Things of Unequal Value

When I lived in that seaside mansion, I encountered a problem. I needed to furnish the place. And I wanted to make it look great. However, I didn't want to spend $100,000 furnishing and decorating it. My wife and I set about this task in several different ways. First, we hit estate sales in wealthy neighborhoods. I'll talk more about this in the following chapters. Second, we scoured Craigslist. This was fruitful in several ways. For one thing, it landed us with some beautiful furniture at bargain prices. More importantly, it also brought us to the home of a wealthy couple which had just refurnished their home, completely changing their style. This meant, of course, that they were liquidating their old furniture. As luck would have it, their old furnishings fit the style of our new place like a charm.

We walked around their garage, examining the various things for sale: a giant rug, an ornate dresser, a couple of antique chairs, a side table, and many more things that would be ideal for our new Spanish home. While we chatted, they learned that we owned a vacation condo on the beach. That piqued their interest. They asked how much it would cost to rent a weekend during the month of March. We calculated four nights at about $1,600. They went on to tell us that they needed to rent just such a condo for their daughter's birthday. They asked if we would take $1,600 worth of furniture for four days in our condo. We immediately agreed.

The result? We landed a bunch of furniture and didn't pay a dime. It wasn't free, mind you. We did let them use our condo for four nights. However, March is a slow month in our condo, and those four nights may have never rented at full price.

This trade is an example of what I call "trading things of unequal value." The value of my condo during an off-season weekend is not actually $400 a night. It's worth less than that because of the odds that it might not rent. So when I trade it for something at full price, I'm getting a higher value for it.

The parties on the other side have the same situation. Their used furniture is not really worth $1,600, because they might not ever receive their asking price for it. They might get just half of that if they sit around and wait for another buyer. When they sell it to me for $1,600, they are getting a higher price than the underlying value of the furniture.

But because each of us gets the full value of our trade, we both come out ahead.

Let's try another example. I'm an attorney. My time is worth $400 per hour. My client sells cigars and humidors. He has a humidor that is worth $400. I want the humidor. If we trade one hour of my time to write a contract for his business, and he pays with the humidor, then we've traded things of unequal value.

The humidor did not cost him $400, but more like $100. The wholesale price that he pays is far below the retail price of $400. Get it? He's buying $400 in services that he only pays $100 for. That means he's getting a good deal, and making his money go further. He's trading something of unequal value (it has more value in the trade then what he actually paid for it).

It's the same on my side. I bill $400 for an hour of my time. But it doesn't cost me $400 because I have extra time that is available. I can use that excess hour of my time that would probably go unsold to other clients; I deploy that hour to trade for a humidor. The hour of my time is worth less than the full $400 because I have more unused capacity.

As long as each party is trading at a higher value than their cost, then they both get a deal. It's the ultimate win-win. If you can sell every hour of your time, then you can't trade things of unequal value. You can still trade your time for something you want. But it will only be a straight trade of your time for something you want.

Sometimes the currency you use is a thing; sometimes it is your time.

If you are a sales rep for a wetsuit company, and you can buy wetsuits for half price, you can trade a wetsuit that costs you $100 for something worth $200 — for example, a person who creates a logo for your website. You get a $200 logo, and the logo artist gets a wetsuit worth $200. But the wetsuit only cost you $100, and the logo artist isn't really spending $200 on the wetsuit because her spare time is worth less than the $200 she charged. Both get something worth $200, while each pays less than $200.

I know of a sales rep for a clothing company who can buy samples cheaply, and is prohibited from selling them. But she can trade them for things. She's traded her samples for watches, shoes, dining out, and many other things that have real value to her. Likewise, I know of a guy with a cabin in the mountains. He trades the use of his cabin for the use of other people's properties for his vacations. I also know a guy with a small restaurant who trades gift certificates to his restaurant for things he wants to buy. Restaurants and bars often trade gift certificates for advertising. I'm a partner in a luxury shoe company. My partner has traded custom shoes for expensive watches. He trades at full retail value. A pair of shoes might retail for $3,500, but have an actual cost basis half of that. When he trades $3,500 shoes, he did not spend

$3,500 out of his pocket. What about the guy who trades him the watch? The watch guy is in the same boat. The watch guy may have paid $1,500 for a $3,500 watch. Each gets something worth $3,500, but each only paid about $1,500.

I've traded my services as an attorney for stock in new business ventures. You don't need to be an attorney to do this. Many startups need help from marketing experts, engineers, web and software developers, ad buyers, and graphic artists. If you are a service provider with extra unsold time, you can use that time to trade for stock in someone's venture. That investment may pay off far more than the amount you paid. And remember that what you paid is an unequal trade: you didn't really pay full price for the stock. By using your unsold time, you are buying it at a discount.

Here's an example. A web developer trades $20,000 worth of her time for stock in a startup. The startup issues stock of that value to the developer. Since the web developer used unsold time to perform the work (think non-billable or "off hours"), it means that the time was not truly worth $20,000 to her anyway. I'm not claiming her unsold time has no value. It may have a value of $10,000 or it may have a value of zero, but whatever it is, the cost to the developer is well under the $20,000 invested. If the company succeeds and eventually sells, the developer will get paid for the stock. And if we assume the company sells at five times the original value, then the developer will get $100,000 from an investment that did not even cost the developer anywhere close to $20,000.

And let's not forget the company is also getting a good deal: It has stock that it would otherwise need to sell to an investor to raise the $20,000 to pay the developer. Of course, the stock is not really worth $20,000 because the startup has no intrinsic value. Moreover, if the company sells stock to an investor and then turns around and pays the developer that $20,000, the transaction requires other costs (transactional costs) that might not be as high with the stock trade. The company also has more stock than it can sell. This means the cost to the company of trading is lower than $20,000, but it is getting the full $20,000 worth of web development work.

So what do you have that you can trade at "unequal value?" Do you cut hair? Then trade that for advice from an attorney, or your CPA for filing your taxes. Do you sell retail goods? Trade them at full retail, which means you are trading something that cost you half of what you are getting in the trade.

When you have a product or service to offer, you can find ways to create currency from that and get other things you may want or need without having to come "out of the wallet" for everything.

To effectively use this type of cashless currency, think outside the box. Consider what you can do with your time, or what goods you have access to, that you can trade. For me, it might be legal services, or business consulting, or letting someone use my vacation condo. For others, it might be teaching music lessons in trade for landscape work, or to trade graphic art for concert tickets. You might know how to program or build web pages, or create digital graphics. You might build cabinets, clean pools or do bookkeeping. Whatever you have in your back pocket, consider ways you might trade that for something you would otherwise pay cash for.

Let's move to the next cashless currency concept.

Shifting

"Shifting" is my label for taking money that would go to one place (such as the IRS) and using it for another purpose. I gave you an example of shifting when I moved out of my condo, rented it and used the excess profit to offset the cost of my rent on a nice house. That was a shift.

I once owned a Mercedes ML320; it's an SUV that costs about $50,000 new. My friend was selling it after just three years for $21,000. A vehicle that weighs over 6,000 pounds qualifies as a work truck under IRS rules. That means a business can buy a 6,000-pound truck and write the entire vehicle purchase off as long as the truck is used more than 50% for business purposes (check with your CPA to be sure the rules are still effective and apply to you).

When I bought this truck, I expensed the entire purchase as a business expense and saved $7,000 in taxes. That made the purchase $14,000 for a three-year-old Mercedes.

My buddy also let me make payments on the car. I gave him $7,000 up front, and paid the rest over two years. And as I said, I saved $7,000 in taxes that same year. I was into the car for $0. I had shifted to myself what I would have paid the IRS, and used it to buy a nice Mercedes. I still paid $7,000, but instead of paying it to the IRS, I paid it to my buddy Ron.

Rich people are masters of shifting. They are particularly good at shifting when it comes to taxes. They use shifting to take money they would owe in taxes and instead use it for investments, real estate, vehicles, and even private jets. They use elaborate shifting mechanisms that go way beyond the scope of this book. Just one example is that the wealthy can create their own insurance company and save millions in taxes, shifting what they would have paid the IRS to pay for their own insurable expenses.[51] Another example is that a wealthy person can buy or lease an electric vehicle, and then qualify for a huge discount on their monthly electric bill. I heard about a guy who lived in a mansion in Rancho Santa Fe, California who had a $2,000 power bill each month. He leased an electric Fiat for $60 per month. Then he applied to the power company for a reduction on his power bill for owning an electric car. The result? His power bill dropped to $1,200 a month. He saved $800 monthly by leasing a car for a mere $60 a month.

For those of us "little guys," shifting requires more creativity. My story of the Mercedes is a small victory. Another one is real estate. As you will remember in Chapter 8, you can save thousands of dollars per year by owning rental income property because of

---

51 The Definitive Guide To Captive Insurance Companies: What Every Small Business Owner Needs To Know About Creating And Implementing A Captive Peter J. Strauss J.D.

depreciation. This represents one of the biggest shifting opportunities for a middle class American.

Once you own a business (or even a side gig), you can deploy a variety of additional strategies to shift what you might pay from ordinary personal expenses to tax-deductible business expenses. These include business travel, office expenses and business meals, not to mention the costs associated with your mobile phone, Internet service, your car and many other deductible business expenses.

While most shifting strategies take advantage of the tax system, there are other ways to shift. For example, I know of a guy who works for a large company. That company pays for his business travel. This guy has a side gig that requires him to meet with clients in various locations around the country. He schedules all his side gig meetings at the same time as his travels for his employer. This means the employer is essentially covering the cost of his travel and meals. That's masterful shifting. Not only does my buddy get to perform his job for his employer, but he's able to conduct meetings and business with his side gig clients as well. He's shifted a major expense that would have cut into his side gig income, but instead has increased the profitability of his side gig. None of this costs his employer in any way, but it provides my friend a substantial financial benefit.

Shifting can also mean looking for ways to avoid paying for what you don't want or need. Instead, you re-focus that money toward something you do want. When I was in law school, I needed to take six units of course work during the summer of my first year.

The tuition was going to cost $8,000. During that summer I would also need to pay my living expenses. One day I was walking through campus and noticed a poster for a "study abroad" program. It had a photo of a college at Oxford University. There was a date, time and room where an informational meeting would be held.

I showed up at that meeting with no hope that I could afford to spend a summer at Oxford. I was a starving student, after all, with a wife and three-year-old daughter. However, the professor in charge of the program explained something remarkable: Tuition abroad at this college cost exactly half as much as what I was currently paying for the same number of units at my law school.

I sat down and did the math with the professor. I would need to pay $4,000 for tuition, rather than $8,000. So far, so good. But I would also need to rent a house in Oxford for my family, pay for travel, housing and meals. Well, the budget for those items was less than $4,000. This means I could spend a summer at Oxford for less than the cost of tuition and living expenses in San Diego. And, of course, I would get to live in England for two months and study at one of the oldest universities in the world — all without having to leave my family.

That's how I took my family on our first trip out of the U.S. We lived in Oxford and it remains one of the most amazing experience of my life. I studied at Magdalen College for that summer. It was where C.S. Lewis taught, where Oscar Wilde was a fellow, and where The Wind in the Willows was written. As a student, I was even given a key to the campus! It was a skeleton key, probably older than I was. I had the privileges of a university student, and could take the college's boats out for a punt along the River Cherwell.

Magdalen College dates to the 1500s (its "new" buildings are 200 years old). I studied European Union law with one of the professors who was part of the movement to create the European Community. I took daily breakfast in a wood-paneled hall with original paintings that dated back hundreds of years, the faces of monarchs looking down upon us as we prepared for the day. I dined at the Inns of Court in London with judges and barristers wearing traditional robes (though no wigs, unfortunately). I had countless wonderful experiences, all while paying less than I would have attending far less fascinating summer courses at home in the U.S.

Meanwhile, my daughter attended preschool and made friends with English toddlers. My wife and I rode bikes to local locks, where boats moved slowly through tributaries that splintered through Oxford. We toured ancient campuses, castles, chapels, and cathedrals. We had pints of beer at the Eagle & Child (aka, the "Bird & Baby"), where J.R.R. Tolkien met weekly with C.S. Lewis. We biked through vast university parks and along the river, and dodged out of the rain under giant willow trees around the university campus.

How did I get this amazing summer studying at Oxford? All I had to do was shift. I shifted the same money I would have spent for a vanilla summer school program and traded it for one of the greatest experiences of my life. Had I not come across the Oxford flyer that day, my $8,000 could still have certainly fulfilled my six-unit requirement adequately here at home. But by opening my mind to another possibility, by shifting that $8,000 ... well, suddenly not only had I fulfilled my six-unit requirement, but I'd also bought myself the experience of a lifetime.

I'm not the only one doing this. Many students today are figuring out how to do this, too, enrolling in full-degree programs and living abroad for a full year.

Deborah was a server at the local microbrewery in my neighborhood. I'd known her for years, and didn't realize that she had been saving money to pay for college cash, rather than going into debt with student loans. One day, she said that she was moving to Amsterdam to attend college. I was shocked.

"Most people just work part time and go to college here," I said.

"It is nearly impossible to graduate without debt," she said. "I want to experience my education without working, and graduate without debt."

I was impressed with her ambition. But I was even more impressed when I found out she had saved $40,000, and was going to pay cash for her entire three-year bachelor's program. The same degree in the U.S. would have cost her $80,000 to $150,000 (and much more after 20 years of interest payments). She found a prestigious university in Amsterdam with a program that was more affordable, and they wanted to add "foreign" students like

Deborah in order to have a more diverse student body. The university would provide housing, and ensure she had a visa. In fact, her visa would even allow her to work a few hours per week, making a little spending money while not distracting her from her studies.

Deborah worked for three years to save her money, then headed off to study for three more. At the end of six years, she will have a B.A. from a prestigious international university. She will have lived abroad for three years. She will have no student debt. Debora opted out of the typical American education trap and shifted her money away from going into debt 20 years in order to pay American universities for her tuition. She received $150,000 in education for $40,000, and she paid for it up front, saving her another $100,000 in interest. She won't spend her life enslaved by student debt.

Shifting is a non-monetary currency that can provide you with an instant life upgrade. Opting out lets you expand your life. At the outset of this book, I revealed that I am something of a "Debbie Downer" when it comes to expensive weddings. I currently live in coastal San Diego, which happens to have dozens of beautiful oceanfront public parks that allow outdoor weddings at virtually no cost. I would strongly encourage the newly engaged to re-evaluate their wedding plans. Consider the cost of the rings, the "destination" bachelor and bachelorette parties, the rehearsal and wedding expenses and anything else that could be considered superfluous. Instead, take the full wedding budget, and then use half of it for your wedding and the other half for a down payment on a rental property, or a home. You'll be shifting, and you'll still get that beautiful wedding at a seaside park, but you'll also go home to a house that you own (and hopefully one that has an extra unit or a Fonzie Flat!).

Swapping

Trading things of unequal value, discussed earlier in this chapter, is a type of "swap" but one that has a unique advantage because each party's cost is lower than the trade. Where there's no unequal value, it's just a swap. A swap is a cashless currency you use when you trade goods or services. Look for possessions you don't want or need, and then trade them for things you do need. Is your garage full of neglected possessions that might be a trove of items you can swap for things you actually want? Before you go spending real money on more "stuff" consider taking some of your idle possessions and putting them to work.

You can swap your airline miles for something you need, or vice versa.

Swap the use of your house for someone else's house for your next vacation.

Swap the use of a room in your house for something of value (I talked about renting a room in your home through AirBnB in Chapter 10).

You can swap your time. You can swap your things. You can

swap favors that are owed to you. You can swap the junk in your garage. You can swap cars, bikes and bicycles. Think of what you have to offer, and start thinking of that as another form of currency.

I once swapped some old landscape equipment in my garage in exchange for labor by a landscaper. I had a guy do a lot of landscape work I would have otherwise paid cash for, and instead paid with my old landscape equipment I didn't need anyway.

Your old possessions are a currency, and even if you don't get an unequal value for something, you can still use it to swap for goods or services you may want or need.

Entire websites are dedicated to providing a forum for swapping. Check out a few here:

- Swapstyle.com

- Thredup.com

- Homeexchange.com

- Zwaggle.com

- Swap.com

- Swapace.com

- Sharedearth.com

- Zilok.com

- Trashbank.com

- Freecycle.com

- Tradestuff.com

- Barterquest.com

- U-exchange.com

Other websites let you swap the use of your home for someone else's home for vacation. There are websites that exist to let you trade or sell your airline mileage. Of course, Craigslist lets you buy, sell, swap and trade anything, anytime, anywhere. Be creative and don't keep using cash when you can trade something and save that cash as part of your plan for financial freedom.

Your skill, talent, and artistic ability is a currency. What you can teach someone is currency. The art you create is currency. What you can do for someone else is currency. Start making use of these non-monetary currencies to swap for goods or services that you need. Barter your time if that's all you have.

Consider managing someone else's real estate as a swap for rent. For a couple that lives together, this is a good way to use teamwork to move ahead financially. I did this when I was a law student. The work took us a few hours a week and created a rent-free living situation for three years. Such an arrangement can provide a major financial lift, particularly if you take advantage of the other concepts in this book.

Borrowing Things

Let me throw in one more concept, although I really shouldn't need to. It's an old-fashioned notion that no one seems to take advantage of anymore. I call it borrowing. You've heard of it? Of course you have! If you need to drill a hole for a DIY project and you don't have a drill, you don't need to buy one! You can borrow one. My adult daughter lives in Portland and rarely needs a drill. She's better off borrowing it than buying a drill that will just sit mostly unused for years. It seems simple, but this concept is lost in a world where consumer products have become so inexpensive.

Of course, everyone has different needs. When I was growing up we had a garage full of tools, and we needed all of them. That was because we used these tools to fix everything without hiring someone to do it. My dad even used those tools to make cabinets for others (a side gig) as well as building our own kitchen cabinets and saving thousands of dollars. My family did this out of necessity most of my life, and I still fix things when it is within my skill set. Do I own some tools? Sure, but I don't need to keep a table saw in the garage. If I really need one, I can call a friend and borrow one.

Think of all of the things you could live without, and borrow rather than buy.

Be the kind of person who is willing to lend what you have. That way you are a lender of things and can then feel better when you call on friends to borrow something. If you own something precious, or have something of sentimental value, then of course you should not lend it. But think of all the useless things sitting in the average garage, closet or junk drawer. Borrow rather than buy. Loan generously as well.

Fix It Yourself

An important cashless currency is your ability to do something yourself, rather than paying to have it done. I come from a family where we did pretty much everything ourselves. I'm not an advocate of everyone fixing everything. You don't need to rebuild your automobile engines, like we did in my family, or build your own cabinets, or (I'm not kidding) repair your own septic tanks. Talk about a shitty job, yuck! But you also do not want to be that person who hires a professional to do every last thing for you. It's about finding a balance and performing the proper cost-benefit analysis for each of the things you might choose to "DIY."

Let me give you a good example. I don't change the oil in my car. Yes, it's easy. I know how to do it. I have the tools. The reason I don't do it myself is because the labor portion of an oil change at the mechanic is about $20. The other costs of an oil change are the same whether I do it myself, or whether I have a shop do it. If I change my own oil, it will take me an hour, and probably make an oily mess in my driveway (another hour to clean up) and I have to find somewhere to dispose of my old oil (two hours of my time to hunt that place down and drop off the oil). I'm in that job four hours and I'll probably cut a knuckle loosening the drain plug on the oil pan. It would be stupid and unprofitable for me to do all of that to save twenty bucks.

Changing brakes is another story. The dealer charges $1,600 to do brakes on my Mercedes SL500. I can buy the parts for about

$250. The total time for me to change all four brakes is about four hours. It's actually about two hours, but I always take longer and end up taking a break to drink a cold beer halfway through. In four hours of my time I'm saving $1,350. When I'm done, I'm done. No mess on the driveway. No jug of oil to recycle. Of course, it might be embarrassing for many people to change their own brakes. I don't mind being the odd man on the street. In fact, I think my wealthy neighbors need a little wake-up call. If you've ever replaced brakes on your car, you know what I mean. To get the disc off, you use a short-handled sledgehammer that requires several loud "gonging" whacks to release the disc.

"Everything okay, Dana?" my neighbor once asked, as I swung my sledgehammer for another blow against the underside of my Mercedes.

"Yeah! All good, just getting the discs off, be done in a bit," I shouted back. They probably think that people living in $2 million homes do not sledgehammer their brake discs on Sunday mornings. This one does.

How do you assess what you should fix yourself and what you should pay someone else to do? I start with the pure economics: What is the total savings by doing it myself compared with what I might do with that money? For me, it's not worth it to change my own oil, wash my own car, or even perform a tune-up. But it is worth my time to change brakes and, in some cases, do heavier auto work. I helped my daughter change her radiator once. It took an hour and it saved $500.

The second part of the analysis relates to your time. How much time do you have? And what is that time worth? If you are a programmer and can bill $200 per hour, and you are fully booked with work, then you should use that calculation in determining what you should pay others to do.

If you're a psychologist who can fix your own plumbing, but it will take you three hours to do so, then you will be spending $600 in your time to fix the plumbing. The plumber might do the job for $200 and guarantee it to boot. Thus, a busy professional might be better off calling the plumber. If you make $20 an hour, then your three hours could be well spent fixing your own plumbing, rather than paying $200 to a plumber. You'll have to work for 10 hours to pay the plumber, and it only costs you $60 in your time to fix it.

The third part of the analysis is self-evident: Do you even know how to do the job at hand? I know a guy who refused to learn how to do anything mechanical so that he would never have to do anything mechanical. That's idiotic. Don't choose ignorance to save yourself from doing hard work. If you are not curious enough to want to know how to fix something, then you should close this book right now, go back to your day job, and forget about being resourceful and finding financial independence. If you willfully choose ignorance, I can't help you with anything. If you are willing to learn, then fixing things is within your reach. I know how to change brakes, but I still watch a YouTube video each time before I put jacks under my car. There are hundreds of other things you can learn to do that will save you money and make you feel great about yourself at the same time.

I understand that not all people are mechanically inclined. Push your limits and learn, but don't do something that is out of your capabilities. That'll only cost you more in the end. But you can save thousands of dollars every year by being wise and fixing things yourself, within a reasonable scope of your capabilities.

When it comes to being a DIY sort of person, don't be the kind who shirks responsibility for basic repairs. But don't go too far the other way and try to fix every possible item either. Find a balance. Repair what you can easily and without risking any expensive mistakes. Become a student of repair, and look for ways to save money for years ahead. Embrace your inner handyman or handywoman.

Recap

Let me recap the non-monetary currencies.

You can trade things of unequal value by taking a product or service you have, and then trading it for its full value. If you give someone a $50 haircut, and they give you a $50 plumbing repair job, then you've traded something of unequal value; at least as long as you have more time to trade.

You can shift by taking an expense you need to pay, and then shifting it from one type of expense to another. The most common way is shifting what you would normally pay the IRS to a tax-deductible expense. In Deborah's case, education provided an opportunity to shift by finding cheaper programs, particularly overseas.

You can swap your time, or swap goods that you may have rotting in your garage. Those items you have purchased but don't want or need anymore are currency for getting what you want.

You can borrow, just like old-fashioned neighbors who need a cup of sugar. Loan what you don't value highly, and borrow when you need a ladder, or tool to change your brakes. I recently borrowed a tent to go camping because I only camp occasionally. It wouldn't be wise of me to purchase a new tent when I only camp once or twice a year.

Finally, you can use your hands and your head to DIY certain projects that would otherwise require cash. Between shifting, swapping, trading things of unequal value, borrowing and DIY, you can expand your life without shrinking your bank account. Use these other currencies and save your cash!

Chapter Twelve:
Scavenging

Scavenging is the third expense pillar. I'll recount a story that might make you think I'm icky. It's a trash digging story. But stick with me through this chapter. The principle of scavenging is looking for opportunity where others kick it to the curb. I'll show you examples that seem beneath you. By the end of this chapter, you'll see how scavenging gets you the good life. Don't picture yourself driving down the alley, pulling stuff out of dumpsters. Picture yourself wearing expensive clothes, driving luxury cars, owning a business, and living the good life. That is what scavenging can get you.

A few years ago, I was setting up a new workstation for one of my employees. I had cobbled together one of the old computers from the office, upgraded the memory and hard drive, and just needed a new monitor. My wife said, "Honey, just grab a new one at Fry's Electronics on the way to the office and be done with it."

Her advice is always spot on. For $100, I could just go get a monitor at the local computer warehouse store. But I'm cheap. And sometimes I prove her wrong (not very often, actually). I thought I'd try a little scavenging before buying a monitor. After all, the computer itself was made of leftover pieces of old computers. Why pay full price for a new monitor?

I had to run to our beach condo that day to drop something off. It was late spring. In the Pacific Beach section of San Diego, there's a major shift that happens in the late spring. College students clear out for the summer and head back home. For scavengers like me, springtime brings a fresh crop of opportunity with every trash day. In fact, students who are moving out often fill the front of their building with "trash" well in advance of trash day. They just put their old furniture on the curb and hope someone will take it away.

I headed south, passing through Pacific Beach, and intentionally drove through the side streets and alleys. Within 10 minutes I saw just what I was looking for. There, on the corner in front of a large apartment complex was a pile of trash, an old sofa, and, wait for it … a 17-inch computer monitor.

I pulled over, loaded it into my Mercedes sedan, and drove to the office. I plugged in the computer, added the monitor and bam! It was in perfect working order. A free monitor for my hacked-together computer. The law clerk using the computer didn't care if the monitor was new. For the record, I never told her that the monitor was literally pulled from the trash just minutes before!

Why would someone throw away a perfectly good monitor? The students have to move. They probably have laptops. They can't pack an old monitor. They can't take it with them. Selling it is not quick and easy. Thus, students tend to leave many valuable things in the wake of their annual return home.

People all over America kick their scraps to the curb. Sometimes they do it literally, as in my example here, in which I took something from the actual curb (no, there weren't old banana peels and cigarette butts on it either). Items people kick to the curb are not in the literal trash. You just have to look a little harder than I did that day. I don't expect my readers to become urban survivalists, and spend their time digging in actual trash. But my example is obviously more than a metaphor. You have to look for opportunity in what others view as trash, and sometimes that may mean finding a monitor on the curb. Most of the time, it means looking where people have lost interest or don't value things (such as students who are moving for the summer). I mentioned earlier in this book that famed investor Warren Buffett looks for "used cigars" when he's shopping for good investments; he scavenges for entire companies that have been kicked to the curb. Whether you're scavenging a computer monitor or a whole company, the strategy can elevate your lifestyle without costing you any additional cash.

Scavenge a Car

Take my Mercedes sedan. You read the story of how I bought a Mercedes SUV, for an effective price of about $14,000 in Chapter 11 (writing off the car and saving $7,000 in taxes). I also purchased a Mercedes E320, a four-door sedan, which cost $50,000 new. I bought the E320 when it was three years old for $17,200 and I swear, it still had the new car smell. Why would someone sell a car that had nothing wrong with it for a third of what they paid? Because it's their scraps. They've moved on to something newer. If they owned a new Mercedes, they've probably opted into the American rat race. If they are rich, then that's fine too. I'll take the car that the rich guy has kicked to the curb! I want to have a life full of nice things, and yet not be stuck, endlessly running on the hamster wheel. Most people buy new stuff and then get rid of it. Use this to your advantage. There's always someone getting rid of something nearly new that they paid full price for. Opt out of buying new.

Once you know that you can have a $50,000 car for $17,200, would you ever want to go to the dealer and pay full price? Of course not! Thus, scavenging is not really about looking for freebies in the trash. Looking for unique opportunities lets you get what you want at a price that is affordable.

How did I get my Mercedes E320 for so cheap? Scavenging. I was looking for something that was being kicked to the curb. The seller had it listed for three months, starting at $25,000. I watched the price drop on Craigslist for those three months, and finally went to see the car when the price hit $19,000. It was the end of the year. The seller operated a small business selling used cars. He had held it for too long and just needed to move it and make room for other cars in his little warehouse. So when I offered $17,200, he took it. I just had to be patient, and wait for the deal I wanted.

How about a free Mercedes? Well, sort of free. I had helped a client many years ago with an expensive case, and the client ended up owing me about $12,000. I let the debt ride. The client was in a business that would, in time, have an up cycle. Eventually, the client and I got together and talked about the debt. He still didn't have the money to pay me. But he had a proposition. He had a used Mercedes CLK500 that he was thinking of selling. It was probably worth $18,000 (new it was $65,000). He offered to just give me the car in exchange for wiping out what he owed me. I took the deal and drove away in a beautiful convertible Mercedes Cabriolet.

I sold that car and bought an even more exotic car. An older gentleman was selling his 2003 Mercedes SL500. A new SL500 costs about $100,000. This one was 14 years old, but had only 24,000 miles on it. I nabbed it for $17,000. I now drive a car that would cost six figures new, and I paid the price of a cheap Hyundai. I can attest that driving an SL500 is very fun, and it's even more fun to know that I didn't have to pay $100,00 for it.

Cars aren't the only thing that you can scavenge. You just need to open your eyes, and start looking in the right places.

Garage sales, estate sales, swap meets and Craigslist are excellent places to find scraps that people are kicking to the curb, particularly in affluent communities. If you don't live in an affluent community, then go outside of your area and scavenge where the affluent live. America is a nation of consumption. People buy new things every day, at full retail price. It is totally foolish. But they do. And the result is that they leave a pile of perfectly good scraps in their wake. It is a wonderful time to be a scavenger. If you want to have nice things, and still claw your way out of moderate American poverty, then you'll need to learn to practice the scavenging strategy. The reason most people don't scavenge is that they lack patience. They want immediate gratification. If you want to get ahead, then you must tame your inner impulsive consumer. Opt out of consumerism. Opt into buying what others have cast aside. We get to live the good life by free-riding on others' consumerism.

Thrift Store Shopper

In the year 2000, I used every dime I had to buy a small but classy house in Las Vegas. It was on a golf course, which turned out to be a good decision (it doubled in value in three years). The purchase left me with an empty, though beautiful, house. I could furnish the house by charging expensive furnishings on a credit card, or I could channel my inner scavenger. I did the latter.

First step: window coverings. You've probably seen people who get their first house and resort to using those silly paper accordion coverings. Yup. Had those. Hated them. First stop: a thrift store where I found beautiful curtain rod brackets and finials for a few dollars (new in the box). The thrift store didn't have curtains or rods. I shopped around. Curtain rods at the hardware store were expensive! Instead, I bought a can of gold paint, a can of black paint and went to the pipe supply warehouse and paid ten bucks for a giant piece of pipe. I channeled my inner HGTV, and created antique-looking elegant curtain rods. A friend with access to cheap textiles found us curtain material and we sent them to a seamstress to stitch. For almost nothing, we now had thousands of dollars in curtains throughout the house. TV: $25. Down sofa: $400 new from a friend with connections to the design industry. Giant expandable name brand table: $80 at a thrift store plus a month in the garage sanding and refinishing it. Kitchen stuff: you name it, we found it at the Goodwill. We purchased a new Henckels knife set for $5 (retail: $400). Expensive new pots and pans: $25. One of the Goodwill stores near us was the recipient of new items that were "returns" from Macy's department store. That provided new home furnishings for about 80 percent off the retail price. Bookshelf: $40 in wood and my labor. I could go on. In a few months and for relatively little money, we furnished the house, painted the interior ourselves and made it a showpiece. Not bad for a first-time homebuyer.

Household items are an easy one for scavengers. You can furnish a house with the things that others paid full price for. I have an old journal entry with a list of at least 50 things I bought at the Goodwill to furnish my first home. All of it was pennies on the dollar. I furnished a classy house with classy things. At the end of the day, I didn't go into debt to furnish my house.

The trick to scavenging is location. The Goodwill store near a university will have high fashion at rock bottom prices because students buy the latest fads, and then unload what they don't want at the local Goodwill. Thrift stores in a city like Beverly Hills may have expensive cutlery for cheap, thousand-dollar shoes, and may even have new items that are from mall stores (often only the packaging is damaged). In the San Diego region, garage sales in La Jolla and Rancho Santa Fe are great for luxury goods, high quality furniture and antiques. I once tripped across an estate sale in San Francisco when I was there for business. I acquired two crystal wine decanters for ten bucks each that would cost $400 new. Shop where the rich live and die.

If you want to go from moderate American poverty to financial freedom, you will need to set aside your pride and your unwillingness to hit the thrift store and pop some tags. You don't have to buy used socks at the thrift store! But you should start to think twice before ever buying something new. Lawnmower: get one at the swap meet or on Craigslist. If you live in Southern California and want to take a weekend in the mountains, you don't need expensive snow chains. Hit the thrift store. Snow chains are one of those things that we San Diegans buy and use once and then dump when we clean out the garage. When I lived in the $2 million house on the bluff over the Pacific Ocean, my house was furnished entirely with used furniture. People loved my Italian leather sofa and chair. They should have; the set cost $12,000 new. I paid $1,200 at an estate sale.

Why do people feel the need to buy new? Two reasons, in my view. One is that people buy things to feel good. It's consumer therapy. They feel happy or rewarded, at least for a little bit. Second, people buy things new because they are too busy to be resourceful. Why shop Craigslist for a new sofa when it's so much quicker and easier to just go buy one at the furniture store?

If you want to break free financially, you cannot just buy everything new. Your money is hard-earned, and you need to deploy your cash toward financial freedom, and not toward possessions. Your "stuff" will just go down in value over the years ahead. Don't waste your valuable cash on things that make you happy for a few days and then go down in value. Invest in your future happiness instead. Use that cash for investing in your side gig or a business that will make you money for many years, and let that help you achieve financial independence.

Remember how I bailed out to live in Bali for 14 months? Before moving to Bali, I held an estate sale to sell most of my worldly possessions, including that Italian leather sofa. I kept only those possessions that I could fit into a 10-by-10 storage unit. I had purchased all my possessions as I describe above (that is, I scavenged them). Then, when I went to sell them, I didn't have any personal ego attached to the possessions. They didn't own me. They were easy to part with. Also, when I held that big estate sale

235

and sold all my belongings, I made $18,000. I estimate that those possessions only cost me about $9,000. Because I had purchased everything used and cheap, when I sold them, I made money. That Italian leather sofa that I paid $1,200 for sold for $2,400.

Scavenge Fashion

How about high fashion? I've scavenged suits. I bought 15 (yes, fifteen) Brioni suits worth $3,500 each. They were new, but had been tailored for someone else. Maybe they were tailored wrong, or maybe their original owner had passed away before putting them to use. In any event, I paid $40 each at a Goodwill Superstore near an affluent neighborhood. I got $52,500 worth of suits for $600.

I've paid $40 for Ferragamo shoes worth $500. My ties, scarves, belts and dress shirts come from a funky store in Arizona that gets all of the returns from Nordstrom stores. Scavenging doesn't mean you have to look like you got dressed at a thrift store. You might see me in a suit and think I spent thousands. If you were to look on the back of my $150 silk tie, you might see $4.99 written in ink on the inner lining!

For the past 20 years, I have worn a name-brand leather motorcycle jacket. The jacket would have cost $600 at retail. It still looks good and I still get compliments. I've easily gotten $600 in use out of it. But, I paid just $59 for it. My wife loves purses and handbags that cost $500 and up. I think the most she has paid for one of her handbags is $79 because she shops used and rarely buys new. My London Fog raincoat, like new and fully lined, was ten bucks at an estate sale and probably never used. I don't need it much in San Diego, but it's great for a business trip to San Francisco or New York. It is classy, and would have cost hundreds of dollars. Even simple things in my wardrobe are from estate sales, garage sales or otherwise second-hand. My valet (a men's jewelry box of sorts) came from a lavish home that was hosting an estate sale. My brass shoe horn was from a flea market in London. I acquired my cufflinks collection from a dozen different estate sales and second-hand stores. My stylish bamboo cane umbrella (rarely used in sunny San Diego) was $1, and may have cost as much as $150 new. My name brand belts came from a sample sale at the local swap meet. Again, "shop where the money lives (and dies)" if you want to find lovely possessions at a great value. You don't necessarily need to travel to Beverly Hills to look at thrift stores and estate sales. There's probably an affluent area near you. It can be fun and profitable to travel somewhere to get a great deal. That's why I go to Phoenix, Arizona every couple of years. Send me an email if you want the name of my secret spot there.

Scavenge Sporting Goods

I don't golf much, but when I do, I play with Ping branded clubs, a Ping bag, and name brand shoes, new gloves, and plenty of expensive golf balls. You guessed it: swap meet for the clubs. Play it Again Sports for the shoes. The gloves were from an estate sale, new and still in the packaging. Divot tools were promos that were free. My bag of tees came with the used bag, along with about fifty golf balls. I didn't need to spend $1,000 on golf stuff. Spending more won't improve my game — I'm a hack! The same goes for my tennis equipment, camping gear, and other sporting goods. You can get all these things that were purchased new by others and then tossed to the curb for pennies on the dollar, ready for those who were willing to scavenge a bit.

Scavenge Business Opportunities

One of the most surprising things people kick to the curb are businesses. I told you in Chapter 5 about how to steal a business (i.e. take over a business with little or no money down). In my own life, four of my businesses have been a result of what someone else kicked to the curb. Why do people toss their businesses aside? Businesses are tied to humans, and humans have problems. Partners end up in disagreement. Business owners have personal or financial problems. In many cases, a business owner has other more successful things to focus on. These provide an opportunity for you to jump at something that has been kicked to the curb. Let me tell you about the four businesses that I acquired by scavenging.

My very first business was a simple landscape maintenance company. I mentioned this business earlier in this book but will explain it in more detail here. I was 19 years old and a sophomore in college when I started Cricket Lawn Care. I started the business with a used lawn mower and other cheap tools, and ran the business from my Volkswagen hatchback. I started that little business from scratch, bootstrapping with just $500 in used equipment. But in order to grow the business, I took over a company that someone else was kicking to the curb.

I had been mowing lawns for about six months. After each job, I would often put flyers on the mailboxes of the customer's neighbors. In one case, I was maintaining the smallest house on one of the nicest streets in a town called Yorba Linda (known as "the Land of Gracious Living," a rather wealthy suburb). The small property seemed hardly worth my time, but for my one-man lawn care business, I needed all the income I could generate. No job was too small! One day, after mowing the tiny lawn, I walked the street and posted flyers on the mailboxes of all the mansions along the same street. Later that night, a man called and asked me to come bid his landscape maintenance. The next week I went to his address. It turned out to be the largest house on the block. It was a mansion with a koi pond, golf putting green and sand pit volleyball court. The owner had fired the previous landscape and was looking for a replacement.

I bid the maintenance of his estate, and won the contract. It was a big win for my little landscape startup. What came next was even better.

About a month after I started taking care of the mansion, I received a phone call. It was the previous landscaper I had replaced!

When I realized who it was, I became nervous. Why was he calling me? It turned out he wasn't calling me to cause trouble; he was calling to offer me a deal. He invited me to his home to meet and talk through it. Within a few days, I showed up to his beautiful home in Orange County, greeted by matching purebred dogs. He had an RV on the side, and a trailer for his off-road toys. His wife poured us each a glass of iced tea, and we sat down to talk.

It turned out he had built a mid-sized lawn care business of his own that was doing just fine. But he had recently taken a job as manager of a large landscape company, and he was making great money. He tried to keep his own landscape company as a side gig. But over time, he was more and more ambivalent about keeping it. He was earning big money at his new job, and his original lawn business had just become a nuisance to him. When he lost his account with the biggest house on the block (he got fired and I got hired), that signaled to him that he was not long for keeping both his day job and his own landscaping business. In fact, that guy with the big house was actually a relative of his! When family fires family, it's clear that someone isn't doing their job. He got the message and realized he needed to do something, or else his lawn care business would just fold up.

He offered to sell me his established landscape business. I definitely wanted to expand my own business, but I didn't have any money. We discussed various ideas, such as making payments over time. As we chatted, I came upon the idea of taking over his accounts and simply letting him continue to collect all the revenue for a month; and then, after one month's time, I would start billing the customers directly. I told him to sell his equipment to someone else, and let me "buy" his accounts by working for free for one month. He liked this idea and we struck a deal. That day, I took over a business that tripled the size of my own, and it was basically free because the entire business was being kicked to the curb. He didn't need it. He had other things to do. He had bigger fish to fry. For him, making money from me for a full month was a victory. He could extract a bit of value from his business rather than waiting longer and seeing the business slowly dissolve. And for me, the addition of his accounts was a huge boost that paid me for many years.

The second business I started was a coffeehouse. It was 1992, and Starbucks wasn't yet a thing. Gourmet coffee was just coming into vogue. I was only 22, and the idea of owning a coffeehouse seemed like fun, and less work than my landscape business. I kept the landscape business going while I set about opening a coffeehouse. I leased a 1930s house that I would renovate into the coffeehouse.

But I was starting the business on a tight budget. A new dishwasher for a restaurant cost about $5,000. A new refrigerator is about $2,000 (I needed two). The list of things a coffeehouse needs added up to about $60,000 in 1992. I opened the whole business with $12,000. How? I found scraps kicked to the curb. I bought the furnishings from a pie shop that had gone out of business (they advertised in the classified section of the newspaper).

I found used appliances at auctions (used restaurant refrigerators were $200 each, not $2,000). It turns out that when businesses fail, the leftover inventory, furniture and fixtures are liquidated for pennies on the dollar. A competing coffeehouse in the same town had spent over $100,000 before opening, whereas I spent only $12,000. It was 1/10th of the cost and we had all the same equipment. I think my coffeehouse had more charm, and I know it cost far less to open. But in order to make it happen, I had to channel my inner scavenger.

Another business that was kicked to the curb is the plant nursery I took over, which I described in Chapter 6. I took over the nursery for nothing and then turned it around and sold it for six figures. The reason I could take over an entire business for nothing? It was no longer of interest to the owner. He had other businesses that were flourishing and needed his attention. The nursery was trash to him, and treasure to me. Of course, I had to be a scavenger and opportunist, and I had to work hard for many months to turn the nursery into a valuable asset. But in the end, scavenging paid off, and I ended up buying my next business with the winnings from the nursery.

As I've said, there are many reasons that businesses are kicked to the curb. Sometimes it's failure (the coffeehouse). Sometimes, the owner has already moved on and doesn't have the time or desire to monetize the value (lawn care company). Sometimes, the business owner has too many other businesses and the one they kick to the curb is broken, worn out and ready for the junkyard (the nursery). Other times, multiple owners of a single business might be in disagreement and one or more owners are exiting to do other things. Sometimes departing owners just want to walk away with their losses, write it off and move onto other projects that are a better use of their time and money.

How can you find these deals? Most of the time, a selling owner will list the business in some way. Some do that on Craigslist. Others on business for sale websites like the ones I mentioned earlier (BizBuySell.com, BizBen.com, BizQuest.com, Business-Broker.net, and DealStream.com). Often, people hire a realtor and list the business on the MLS. You won't always know if it's an undervalued deal until you take the time to kick the tires. Start your scavenger hunt, and be patient until a deal resonates with you.

Scavenge Real Estate

Even real estate can be an opportunity for a scavenger! I know of one man who happened to find a couple with real estate that they were not happy to own. The story is complicated, and too much to cover here. But I can tell you this much: There was a divorce, a business failure, and a bankruptcy. There was also some random debt against the property. For the divorcing couple, the land had no real equity. But for my friend, it was an opportunity. He managed to take over the property as-is by paying the couple $100,000 and assuming all of the problems tied to the property. He negotiated with the creditors and liens and, in the end, even negotiated with the bank the couple had borrowed from. He ended up owning a valuable piece of property, debt-free, and he paid a fraction of the value because he was willing to deal with the messes. He didn't mind getting his hands dirty. It was just like digging in the trash, buying at a thrift store, or buying a business that is in disrepair. For the scavenger, these are all opportunities. Imagine getting a $400,000 property for $100,000. That can be life changing.

You can't expect those deals to be advertised. You can't wait around and hope one falls into your lap. You must scavenge and look for opportunities. For my buddy, this was a deal he happened to know about because he had his radar tuned, looking for scavenger opportunities. Maybe people will read this book and say, "Show me how" or "Show me where." Here's the reality: the deals will appear when you are looking and listening. If you aren't tuned in, you won't see the opportunities. When I found the property management business, it wasn't because I was actively shopping for a business to buy. A realtor happened to tell me that her friend was selling a business. I was tuned in for opportunities and was able to ask questions and find a deal that I may have missed if I was not paying attention. When I found the seaside mansion, it was because I went to the estate sale to look for bargains, and then asked about renting the house. No one is going to deliver these in a tidy package. It is up to you to tune your radar to the right signals, and become open to this type of opportunity.

I hope you can see that learning to scavenge isn't going to make you a trash digger trying to recover uneaten bananas. The scavenging I advocate is to help you live a better life, and yet reduce your expenses dramatically. You can scavenge for high end fashion, cars, furniture, electronics, and other consumer items and save thousands every year. You can scavenge and end up with a money-making business, or side gig, that not only cost you little or nothing, but generates income for you as well. Even real estate can be scavenged.

I'm sure that some of you will start to notice things in people's trash as you drive down the street. My head turns when I pass something on the side of the road. I'm certainly not above stopping to pick up a tool that may have fallen off someone's truck. But the point of this chapter is to direct that scavenger instinct toward more valuable items, items that will improve your life. You can be a well-dressed gentleman with fancy suits, nice shoes, and an expensive watch, driving a luxury car and living in a mansion, and have done so without spending much money at all. You can also use these same principles to give yourself a life of freedom. Freedom from work, freedom to travel or live abroad. Freedom to live a life that most people only dream of.

Chapter Thirteen: Traveling the World

Mark Twain said, "Travel is fatal to prejudice, bigotry, and narrow-mindedness, and many of our own people need it sorely on these accounts. Broad, wholesome, charitable views of men and things cannot be acquired by vegetating in one little corner of the Earth all one's life."

In my own experience, travel has been transformative. I'm a different person because of my travels.

While a large number of Americans have a passport, only a very small percentage of Americans use those passports to travel overseas. One article states that only 3% to 5% of Americans travel abroad.[52]

This seems accurate based on my experience. Most Americans never travel outside of North America. I'd like to talk about travel

---

52 http://www.huffingtonpost.com/william-d-chalmers/the-great-american-passpo_b_1920287.html

because I think more Americans should travel. And I believe that many people don't travel because they perceive it is more expensive than it really is. I hope that demystifying travel will encourage more people to do it.

Travel brings us into contact with other ideas, cultures, and experiences. Travel will change your life. It will change your worldview. It will broaden your palette. It will make you wiser. It can make you a better person. Most people who live the Opt Out life are travelers. I'd like to push you to travel.

Why People Don't Travel

Most people don't travel for one of two reasons. First, people perceive that travel is expensive. Second, people fear the unknown, including fear of long flights. I'd like to address both the myth of expensiveness and the fears that prevent people from traveling.

Fear

Let's start with the issue of fear. The most common fear is that of being in an unknown land where you don't know the language. This is a rational fear. However, travel doesn't necessarily mean going to remote regions of the Amazon. Almost everywhere I have traveled people speak English, or at least enough English to get by. It is a good time to speak English because English is the language of business and travel for most other people around the world. If a Chinese person goes to Italy, they will get around by speaking English. If a Frenchman goes to Indonesia, he will speak English. Thus, English-speakers have the luxury of traveling almost anywhere in the world and being able to speak our native language.

Of course, learning another language makes travel even more gratifying. I've learned Spanish, and a bit of Mandarin, and Indonesian. Traveling in Spain, Latin America, China, and Indonesia is a bit easier with a basic understanding of the native tongue. But most people who travel will simply rely on their English. I assure you that you can show up in Bali and get around just fine with English. The same goes for Spain, France, Thailand, China, Japan, and well, just about everywhere in the world. I've even been on a tiny island in Vietnam and got around with English just fine. However exotic you want your travel to be, you need not fear the language barrier. In fact, I'll tell you the people I have a difficult time understanding when I travel: British people. Those English, Welsh, and Scottish accents can make it darn near impossible to understand my own ancestors speaking my native language!

That said, before landing in a new destination, it's a good idea to get a little booklet of the local language. People in most countries really appreciate any effort to use their language. When you try speaking their language, it disarms them and they become more generous about using their English. They are far less worried about how bad their English is once they hear you try to speak their language!

Aside from the fear associated with the language barrier, many people fear the unknown. Well, the whole point of travel is to see something you haven't seen. It is to intentionally expose yourself to the unknown. It is okay to have a healthy fear. Fear at one level will keep us from harm. Fear will keep you from wandering down a dark alley in Jakarta. But it should not keep you from going to Jakarta. You are statistically more likely to be robbed in your own backyard than on a trip abroad.

Another thing that keeps people from traveling is the fear of long-distance flights. I suppose the underlying fear is simply the fear of death. The plane may crash. Yes, planes can crash. But the odds are higher of a shark attacking you, or lightning striking you, than of your transatlantic flight going down. So the fear is irrational. If you fear death, then you should be more careful at home or near your home, where most fatal accidents occur. We all have some primordial desire for self-preservation. To live life to its fullest, you are going to have to accept the imminence of death. You are going to die. It is out of your control. You are not going to extend your life by not flying.

Oddly, many of the same people who don't fly out of fear are the same ones who smoke, drink, and eat unhealthy foods and refuse to exercise. These will take years off their lives. Those habits literally will kill you over time. But those same people will refuse to get on a plane.

One of the greatest therapies for overcoming a fear is simple: Just do it. If you fear flying, then fly. If you fear travel, then travel. Face the fears and watch them dissipate! Start with baby steps! Go to England or Australia and practice where English isn't a problem. Try Hong Kong, where English is the second language, or France, where most people have studied English in school. But, by all means, overcome your fear and travel.

You might fear getting robbed. Well, you might get robbed in your own town. The solution to this fear is easy: Just don't go to places where you're likely to get robbed. Seasoned travelers do the same. Study before you travel and then stay on the well-trod roads to avoid getting robbed. You can avoid being scammed if you have done your homework before going to someplace new. Just like you should read more books about business before you buy a business, and read more about real estate before you buy rental properties, you should prepare yourself adequately before you take a big trip.

People might fear getting sick from local food. This can happen, of course. But if you are traveling to places where there is a thriving tourist industry, you'll find plenty of reasonably priced restaurants where the food is good and the kitchen is clean. I've eaten from street vendors in Bali, Bangkok and Ho Chi Minh City and never become sick from it. Your odds of getting sick while traveling are just as high as in your own town.

Now that I've said my piece about travel fears, let me address the myth that travel is expensive. Travel doesn't have to be expensive. Let's talk about traveling the scavenger way.

Travel Isn't Expensive

For many destinations, travel is cheaper than you might imagine.

The cost of travel is ridiculously cheap in Bali, Indonesia, Thailand, Vietnam, China, Cambodia, Philippines, Malaysia, and many other wonderful destinations. In Bali an average meal at a restaurant costs $3. You can rent a motorbike for $5 a day, get a cab across town for $4, or an Uber for a dollar. You can sit down to a fancy meal and only spend $10. A two-week trip to Bali can be had for $750 in airfare, and then another $750 for accommodations, meals and transportation. It is possible. Can you set aside $120 a month? If so, you can travel.

Asia isn't the only cheap place for travel. I've spent extended time in Spain and Italy over the past few years. I can eat a meal in Spain for $5 to $7 if I'm careful. In Spain and Italy, you can eat tapas, pintxos or chiquetti for free if you also order drinks. You can book a small hotel room for $40 a night, including breakfast. There is public transportation, but I've also rented cars for a remarkably low price and have driven all over Spain and Italy.

You can travel to many amazing destinations and find cheap accommodations. Sometimes rooms are cheap and, if you aren't choosy, you can just show up and find a little hotel, hostel, or a room in a local's house, or homestay. Other times you can lock down a deal on VRBO.com or AirBnB and show up to a wonderful home or room that is quaint, clean and affordable. If you want to travel long-term, you can often find deals that are incredibly cheap. On Gili Air, an island off Lombok you can rent rooms for about $30 a night that are rustic, but quite nice. If you want to stay a month, you can negotiate to pay $200 per month. Imagine staying a month on a tiny island for $200, and then only paying

$10 a day for food!

What about that horribly expensive airfare? Well, I've paid $700 for a round trip fare to China. I've paid as little as $400 for a round trip ticket to Europe from the U.S., and $375 round trip from San Diego to Maui. I paid $1,000 for airfare from Indonesia to Paris for a recent business trip. That was nearly halfway around the world (and back) for $1,000. Traveling during off-peak times, or finding last-minute deals can make travel even less expensive. If you are following the principles of this book, you will have a side gig that generates plenty of money to enable you to travel. There are a host of websites that specialize in listing cheap airfare. And, of course, you can use airline miles to make it even cheaper.

Compare Local Travel to International Travel

Some folks may balk at the idea of spending $1,500 for two weeks in Bali. However, those same people view an RV vacation as affordable. Or, they might take a mini-vacation to Las Vegas for a weekend, or maybe Palm Springs. Few of these are as cheap as a trip to Bali. Here's why.

If you take a weekend in Las Vegas, you need airfare. That's $200 from Southern California, but it's about $500 for most of the rest of the U.S. Then, once you are in Las Vegas, you have to pay a taxi to get to your hotel and then of course you pay for the room. Unless you are at a dive hotel, you'll pay $200 and up for a decent room. Food in Las Vegas is no longer a $5.99 all-you-can-eat buffet. Food in Las Vegas is now quite gourmet ... and expensive.

You then pay for nightclub entry, or a show and drinks, and then food or expensive drinks by the pool. Three nights in Las Vegas, with airfare, will be $1,500 per person. And of course I haven't even mentioned the gambling. That same $1,500 will buy you airfare to Bali, and two weeks at a decent hotel or homestay, and all your meals. The Bali trip will change your life, but the Vegas trip will just leave you with a nasty hangover.

Bali is just one example I use because I am so familiar with it. The same $1,500 will get you a life-changing trip to Thailand, Vietnam, Philippines, China, and any number of other exotic destinations. I recently took my father on a nine-day trip to Dublin, London and Paris. Our airfare was free using miles we had earned. But the flight would only have cost $700 if we did not have miles. We shared a $120 hotel in Dublin, a $200 hotel near the Abbey in London, and rented a charming vacation rental in Paris. The Paris unit was a refurbished wine cellar, a spacious flat with a week's worth of coffee pods, and within a short walk to everything, all for $140 per night. Before food, our trip would have cost $1,000 each if we had paid with cash for airfare (rather than airline miles). Our meals were cheap. Breakfast was often free with our room. Lunch would be a stand-up meal for less than ten bucks. Dinner might be a pub for a burger, or an occasional fancy meal. You can get to Europe inexpensively and once there, you can stay and eat cheap if you are up for a little adventure.

The RV Camper
What about the budget traveler who believes that camping is

cheaper? If you want to go camping because you love it, then you should keep on doing it. But, I've known many people who believe that it's cheap. My family camped for both reasons: we loved it, and my parents thought it was cheap.

I'd like to point out that RV camping isn't cheap, not because I want to criticize it, but because I want you to see that world travel is not as expensive as you might think, and by comparison the things you might think are cheap aren't so cheap. Whether you own an RV or rent one, the cost of the RV is substantial. You'll need to fuel your RV, maintain it and pay for insurance. On each trip, you have to stock up on groceries to cook your own food or eat out. In many cases, people do both. That adds up fast. Then you also need camping gear. You need something to do when you camp, so most people buy toys, games, hiking gear, motorcycles, etc. All of this has a cost. Unless you are a basic tent camper, then there is little real cost savings by camping versus taking a trip abroad.

Someone might object, "But I can take my family out for a week and pay only $300 for campsite fees — how is that cheaper than taking a family of four to Europe?" The answer starts with the camper, RV, or trailer. It costs some cash to buy a camping vehicle and then costs more to maintain and insure, and then costs again each time it is used. You can probably get a used RV for $2,500, but for that price, you are going to get a junker that breaks down on the way to the mountains. So, let's go with a used RV price of $8,000. If the RV has a useful life of eight years, then

you are paying $1,000 per year to own it. You then have mainte-
nance of $1,000 per year, assuming you do some of it yourself,
and that you wash it and clean your black water tank yourself.
You'll then insure it, which is another $500 per year, if not more.
When you use it, you must pay for fuel, which at eight miles per
gallon will amount to $100 for a short weekend trip. You'll pay
for a few meals on the road, and then the food you eat while you
camp. If you are a typical nuclear family, mom is going to spend
the whole vacation cooking and cleaning, which according to my
mom, isn't a vacation at all. And if you add all this up, you are
looking at spending about the same to own an RV and camp as
you would spend to take your family of four on a trip abroad
once a year. Again, if RVing is your thing, I'm not against it. It is
just a tool I'm using here to compare the perceived barrier to international travel.

By comparing the cost of domestic vacations to Las Vegas, or RV
camping vacations, you can see that the price for travel abroad is
not more expensive. Frankly, even if it was slightly more expensive, it would still be worth the additional expense, just to experience the benefits of travel. Overseas travel will change you in
ways that domestic travel won't. Do both! If you have a side gig,
and if you rent your house out on AirBnB, you'll have the freedom to do more of everything.

Using Airline Miles
When it comes to being a scavenger, paying for travel can be-

come even cheaper! If you use a credit card or debit card regularly, you can accumulate mileage with an airline that will allow you to travel for less, and in some cases free. There are entire websites and blogs dedicated to helping people maximize the benefits of their air miles. I've applied for credit cards that granted me 50,000 miles just for the application, and then additional bonus miles for using the card right away. What will that get you? I've taken free round-trips to Europe and China for under 50,000 miles.

In addition to accumulating miles when you apply for a credit card, you can get miles for merely using your card. If you use a card for business, or for your employer, then you can really rack up the miles and use those miles for your family's airfare, and even for rental cars. Mileage cards are one of the biggest travel hacks, and if you want to travel on an extreme budget, you'll want to join some of the online communities that focus on that.

Write Off Travel for Business

In some cases, you can write off part or all your travel if your travel is necessary to your business. If you travel on business, you can write off a portion of your travel expense, which is a shifting technique I talked about in Chapter 9. You can shift part of the money you would normally pay the IRS to yourself and your business. I've taken trips that are important to my business. I have important relationships to maintain in many countries, and thus, when I desire to work on those relationships, I can enjoy at least some tax savings on the money spent to travel on business.

Avoid Expensive International Hotels

One of the most important ways to save money on travel is to do your research and figure out how you can stay in the area of a city you want to visit without staying at an intercontinental hotel. In Indonesia, many homes have little bungalows for rent, and some houses have apartments called homestays. These can be a fraction of the price of a hotel. In Spain, hostels are not just divey little crash pads for students. They are often real hotels and quite inexpensive. Of course, student-oriented travel is available, too. If you don't mind bunking with students, then find a youth hostel, where you can rent a bed for 20 Euros and also get to know other travelers more easily. You can even couch-surf for free by joining one of the couch-surfing web communities like couchsurfing.com.

In China on one business trip, I found that fancy local hotels could be reserved for less than $100 per night if a local contact booked the room. So I just ask the person I know in China to make the booking, and then I pay for it on my credit card when I arrive. I've had a few luxurious experiences in China, but you may never find local luxury hotels online because they don't market to English speakers. If you do a little hunting (using Google Translate), you can find a good deal on a locally branded hotel, rather than an international chain. You might get the full luxury treatment for a fraction of what you'd pay if you stayed at an American branded hotel. Pick up some books and find opportunities that others are passing up. Also, consider VRBO and

AirBnB because your host may provide you with some great advice about what to do on your trip!

Eat Cheap

When you are traveling, you have a lot of control over food costs. For starters, don't eat on the main drag[53]! Don't eat on a fancy rooftop deck. Well, occasionally you might choose to splurge. I once ate at the Rex in Ho Chi Minh City because it was a historic landmark. During the Vietnam War, it was the location for the press and military officers, and was a key hub for reporting on the war. Dining there cost four times the price of the best local restaurant, but I chose to experience that particular place as part of my travel experience. For most other meals on that trip, I ate inexpensive local food. I had one of the most amazing local meals in Vietnam for about $3. It wasn't at a seedy vendor at a rickety food cart either (not that I'm above eating street food). It was a large restaurant with English-speaking servers, and they had amazing first-world-quality food. If you want to travel on a budget, you can do it. You just need to use your head, do your research and then explore.

---

53 There are certainly dangers of eating somewhere that makes you sick. I've never been to India, but I hear that nearly everyone from the U.S. gets sick at least once on a trip there. My own philosophy is to eat where there is a high volume of cooking. That way, the food is fresh. If you approach a restaurant that has no customers, you should pass on it.

Vagabonding the World

Some people have taken travel to an even further extreme. They "vagabond" around the world permanently! One of my friends became fed up with life about 15 years ago. He rearranged his life so that he could travel abroad for a year. He paid a bookkeeper to collect rent on his two small properties and pay his bills, and then deposit what was left at his bank. He planned to do this for a year. However, it's been more than 15 years and he's still going strong. Why should he stop? He's vagabonding around the world, living cheap and enjoying life!

He's not alone. I know from spending time abroad that there are many, many people who find a way to vagabond for a month, a year, or permanently. The guy who first turned me onto Bali was a bartender who was bailing out to take an indefinite trip to Bali. He and his girlfriend spent more than a year abroad. They saved while working in the U.S. and traveled close to the earth so they didn't have to work for seven months. They ran low on funds, and went to Australia (which is near Indonesia), where it was easy to get a one-year working visa. They worked for a few months, saved up again, and then spent the last few months back in various parts of Indonesia. They have surfed, hiked, partied, played with monkeys, made friends, had amazing experiences and saw places that very few Americans have ever witnessed. They've had the experience of a lifetime. They are changed by their travels and will never be the same. The cost for this was ridiculously low. They didn't need to sell a business, win the lottery, or inherit money. They saved a bit, and then worked a few

259

months in Australia to save up again and keep the journey going.

I can think of more than a few people who have made travel and side gigs come together in a way that gives them the right balance. Remember my friend Mel who skis every winter and then bounces around Indonesia buying things she sells at street fairs? She has found an equilibrium that is right for her. Another friend of mine is importing purses and sandals from Asia, allowing her to be in various parts of Asia for travel when she wants, and also reside back in the U.S. when she wants.

Some people travel permanently by working for a few months each year and then taking the rest of the year off to live somewhere inexpensive. A person can work on a cruise ship for three months and save enough to live well for a year in most areas of Asia. I've met people with seasonal businesses in the U.S. who only need to be in the U.S. for a few months while they work hard and then they take the rest of the year off to vagabond. You don't need to be rich or retired to travel. You just need to think differently about travel, and about money.

House Swapping

What about the average Joe with a house and mortgage and kids and all of that? If you are the average Joe, you are in luck! One way to travel cheaper is to swap your house for someone else's in another country. There are several large house-swapping sites. I have personal knowledge of two families that have done this, and both were quite happy with the results. One family ended up staying in a historic mansion in a coastal town in France. They let the French family use one of their older cars, so the French family reciprocated. My friends stayed in a French mansion and drove around the French coast in a local car, and saw a part of France no one else had seen from that perspective. The cost was nothing. They came back to find no damage to their house. Why would they? The French family had the same respect, since they were both using each other's homes and cars. The same family used airline miles for the airfare, making their French vacation nearly free. Imagine three weeks in France for the same price as staying home!

You can also rent out your house for the time you want to be gone. You've read about me doing this for $10,000. You might not get that much money for two weeks in your house. But you can put your house up on VRBO or AirBnB or any other rental site and offer a price that is reasonable. What if you can get $2,000 for letting someone use your house for two weeks? If you combine that money with free mileage flights, and inexpensive meals, you can still get a vacation for free.

What about your possessions? What if someone breaks your favorite vase? Ugh. Those damn possessions. Stop worrying about your possessions. If you've acquired everything the scavenger way then you aren't going to stress about whether someone breaks some of your dishes. That wine decanter only cost ten bucks at an estate sale, right? But, sure, if you want to put some things in a safe place, then choose a couple of closets to put locks on, place your precious stuff in those, and lock them up. No one wants your stuff, but if you want to be safe, then simply lock it up and don't worry about it while you are sunbathing on the Mediterranean.

Just Do It

Travel is a part of the transformation you will experience if you start taking on my worldview. You are going to realize that "stuff" has little value, and that experiences have great value. You will shift what you may previously have spent on stuff, or what you spend on cable TV and entertainment, and put that money to use on wonderful experiences that only come from travel.

I have money to travel because I don't spend it on possessions. I rarely buy new things. I don't pay for cable TV, I don't have the latest gadgets and toys. I own suits that I bought for $40 at a thrift store. Not only do I have the money to travel because of the lifestyle I choose, but I also spend less on travel than you would expect, as I detailed above.

You can do the same! As you begin to unravel the old you, you will think before spending needlessly on the things that society says you need, and you'll also start to value experiences more. What do I buy when I am traveling abroad? Not souvenirs. Not trinkets. I buy a piece of street art for my dining room wall. I bring back pockets of seashells that will fill glass jars that adorn my kitchen and bathrooms. There is no need to spend any money on things when I travel. I spend it on experiences — experiencing food, people, places, surfing, sailing, diving, hiking, museums, concerts, and memories that enrich my life, rather than filling a suitcase full of crap that I'll just kick to the curb later at a garage sale, or that my daughter will sell at an estate sale when I'm dead.

Make travel a priority, and learn to do it the scavenger way. You'll have more fun. You'll travel the world, while still building a life of financial freedom, the Opt Out way.

Chapter Fourteen:
Your New Life as a Subversive Millionaire

I've probably sent you into "system overload" with many of the strategies in this book. I hope that you get infected with the same bug I have. Yeah, I sneezed on you, and now you're sick, too. If you've caught this flu, it's going to change your life. It'll start in small ways. You'll be watching less television. You won't shop at the mall. You'll be learning how to run an eBay account, or an Amazon store. You'll be asking people new questions because you'll be looking for your side gig, exploring real estate, and studying business.

Your spouse or significant other is going to notice. Try to get him or her on board! With two partners in crime, you'll be fighting strong forces that want to keep you in moderate American poverty. You'll have to battle inertia, inflation, societal norms, and various other forces that want to keep you stuck where you are.

Keep going back to our strategy. Opt out. Change how you think about everything. Then get on with the practical implementation of the income and expense pillars.

Get a side gig going. It may take time! Be patient. That's going to be your golden goose for many years. After that, slowly work into a business with your bootstraps and your side gig income. If you find a business that's been kicked to the curb, steal it! Bootleg a business and pay the owner over time. Finally, acquire rental property to generate income, save taxes, and grow your future wealth.

Take that home of yours and make it generate income, and use it for trading for your next vacation. Start using your non-cash currencies to make your life more awesome. You'll save your cash, while also getting what you want. And, finally, learn to be a scavenger. Through all of the strategies, you'll be looking for opportunity where others refuse to see it.

Why are more people not scavengers? Pride is one reason. Many people feel that it is beneath them to have second-hand clothes, or second-hand anything for that matter. The psychological barrier is quite high for many people, and this can be difficult to overcome. I came from a blue-collar family. For me, second-hand is second nature. We pass down everything. My daughter wore clothes from her cousins. The cousins received toys and clothing from their cousins. My brother wore my clothes as I grew out of them as a kid. If we needed a lawnmower, we would have purchased a used one, rather than paying full price for a new one. Thus, for many of us, there is no inner, soul-defining meaning that binds us to our possessions, and we certainly have no qualms about slightly used clothes, furniture and appliances.

For many Americans, there is a high barrier that prevents them from owning something that has been used by someone else first. Much of this is driven by marketing. We are raised with advertisements that sell us the lie that we will feel richer if we own this or that. We are told we will be more desirable, sexier, more handsome, happier, if we acquire whatever is being sold. We also believe that others view us a certain way because of what we own. We not only have an internal view of ourselves that is driven by misconceptions about what gives us self-worth, but we also have (or more accurately, perceive) a self-worth that is tied to how we think others view us. What might they think if they knew my suit was from a thrift store?

The truth is, they just might judge me and think less of me. That's fine. I don't derive my personal worth by how others perceive me. Then again, I never advertise the fact that my Brioni suits were from the Goodwill Superstore. I certainly told my closest friends and family. But there was no reason to tell my clients and colleagues. I just had nice suits and looked sharp. Good enough. And look, even if I had bragged about my $3,500 suits being from a thrift store, and others thought that was strange, it would not have impacted how I felt about my own self-worth.

If you are ever going to get out of moderate poverty, you will need to break these mental chains. You can't tie your worth to owning things that corporate America wants to sell you. Your value is not in what you own. It is in the freedom to do what you want, when you want. If you go buy that thousand-dollar handbag right now, you will not suddenly be that beautiful model featured in their marketing campaign. If you wear name brand perfume, you will not find yourself on a yacht on the Mediterranean with a gorgeous half-naked model serving you a cocktail. Drinking Dos Equis will not make you the most interesting man in the world. Break the chains that tie your sense of worth to what you own.

In addition to breaking your internal psychological connection to things, you will need to confront — and change — how others' perception of you influences how you feel about yourself. It will be quite difficult to climb out of moderate poverty if you are worried about keeping up with the Joneses, and even harder if you feel the need to care how the Joneses think of you. Of course, if you are going to be a scavenger like me, you are welcome to be subversive about it. In fact, I encourage you to keep it to yourself! Why give away all your secrets? Obviously, I'm out of the closet, as they say. Publishing a book that shares my stories means I can't fly under the radar any longer. But you certainly may keep your mouth shut when people compliment your amazing new pair of $500 shoes that you purchased for fifty bucks. Others may not have a lower opinion of you for wearing shoes that you purchases second-hand. Either way, it is still better for you to simply diminish the value of what others may think of you, and thus break one of the shackles that keep so many people in moderate American poverty.

I'm encouraging you to shed your need of possessions, to diminish the need to buy new and instead look for scraps, opportunities, deals, bargains, discounts, slightly-used, and downright abused possessions. Instead of feeling proud and boosting your self-worth by purchasing something new and expensive, you can create the same gratification instead by scoring a sweet deal. I don't get a dopamine rush from hitting the mall and buying a new wallet. I get a rush when I find a vintage wallet at an estate sale and buy it for three dollars. I also end up with more money in that new wallet.

We should be happy that the world is full of consumers who are willing to buy new things for full price and then sell them to us for pennies on the dollar. I am happy to see the mall full of shoppers buying. They keep the economy going. They keep stock prices rising! But just because they help the whole economy function does not mean that it is the right path for your financial independence. We must become Opt Outs without becoming dropouts if we are going to be financially independent. We're happy to allow that system keep going, but then are even happier to opt out and become subversives who prey on the waste created by the masses. They're creating a buffer for us, after all, by paying full price. This means we pay far less. I love the four Mercedes that I've owned. But I would not have paid $50,000 to $100,000 for any of them. I needed someone else to pay that price, so that they could become devalued, and then I could swoop in and receive the benefit from enjoying a longer-term ownership at a far lower price. For just one of those cars, its value had dropped from

$50,000 to $17,200 over its first three years. But not for me — that loss was shouldered by the original owner, who bought a new car in the traditional "opt in" way that so many others do. And so for 10 years I was the beneficiary of a car who's value dropped much less sharply when I owned it, in this case from $17,200 to $8,000. That means that for the first three years the original owner suffered a decline of $32,800 — more than $10,000 per year — while during my 10 years of ownership the same car only went down in value each year by only $1,000. That's a 10x difference. That's the Opt Out difference.

We want the rest of the world to keep on blowing its wad on consumption. Let them spend! It's because of their excess that we can live even better lives at a fraction of the cost and still have what we want, while also having the freedom we need to get out of moderate American poverty.

What will your life look like once you opt out?

You'll have a great life. You'll live where you want. You'll have a beautiful home that doesn't stress you out. You'll have a nice car you're proud to drive. You'll own nice things. You won't have credit card debt. You'll own what you own outright. You'll have the freedom to travel. And when you travel, you'll do it with intention and have the experiences of a lifetime.

I want to see you implement my strategies and change your life forever. I want you to live the good life, and then retire well, and leave a legacy for your heirs. I want you to have the freedom to participate in the public dialogue as a strong, independent citizen with money and self-sufficiency. I want you to have the resources to give your time and your money to support causes that will change the world. I want you to become the best version of yourself, using your free time to grow your mind, rather than letting it melt under the rays of your computer screen or television.

I want you to take advantage of tax loopholes that only the rich use, and then deploy that money to create a life of greater freedom and autonomy.

Yes, I want you to have a life that includes the things you want. But in the end, I will have succeeded if you are empowered to live the life that you want.

Follow me at optoutlife.com and continue your journey to the Opt Out Life.

Made in the USA
San Bernardino, CA
15 July 2018